What every parent should know... *before* their child goes to university

What every parent should know…
before their child goes to university

Jane Bidder

Editors Richard Craze, Roni Jay

new tricks for old dogs

Published by White Ladder Press Ltd
Great Ambrook, Near Ipplepen, Devon TQ12 5UL
01803 813343
www.whiteladderpress.com

First published in Great Britain in 2005

10 9 8 7 6 5 4 3 2

ISBN 0 9548219 1 2

British Library Cataloguing in Publication Data
A CIP record for this book can be obtained from the British Library.

Designed and typeset by Julie Martin Ltd
Cover design by Julie Martin Ltd
Cover illustration by Sue Misselbrook
Illustrations by Chris Mutter
Printed and bound by TJ International Ltd, Padstow, Cornwall

White Ladder Press
Great Ambrook, Near Ipplepen, Devon TQ12 5UL
01803 813343
www.whiteladderpress.com

Contents

Introduction

My husband and I will never forget taking our son up to Scotland for his first week at uni. The car was laden with clothes, stereo, computer, plus the odd book and you could just about make out an extremely moody teenager in the back, with a duvet over his head. Conversation was limited and I had flu which meant my map reading skills were worse than usual.

We arrived at his halls of residence – which he'd never seen before – to discover they looked like a giant unwashed liner (despite apparently winning an architectural award some years ago). We weren't allowed in the hall until the afternoon because it was still being cleaned after a conference, so we had to hang around the local town with our still moody teenager in tow. We knew the mood was masking apprehension but it didn't help.

By mid afternoon, we were queuing up with other parents, outside the unwashed liner. To our son's horror, we began talking to another family on the steps in front. It was the best thing we could have done. Their son (less moody) was reading the same subject as ours and turned out to be in the same corridor.

We duly trooped in when the doors opened, to be greeted by a loud member of the halls committee, demanding subs and yelling "Next" at the top of her voice as an indication that we should move along fast. We did – only to find that his room was not much bigger than a downstairs loo into which they had somehow squeezed a bed, a desk and a wardrobe.

Our son took one look and said "Is this what I've worked so hard for?" I could have cried. Instead, we set to cramming as much as we could into the room and taking the rest back to the car. Meanwhile, my husband knocked on the adjacent door and introduced our embarrassed son to a very friendly second year.

We did a quick recce of the laundry and kitchens before our son told us in no uncertain terms that it was time to go and could he please have an extra fifty quid for emergencies. I cried all the way home and my husband – a law abiding citizen – was so upset that he put his foot down on the motorway and was pulled up by a police car. When we told him we'd just delivered our first born to university, his eyes filled with sympathy. "Did that myself last year," he said. "You get used to it – eventually." Then he sent us on our way with a mild warning.

I didn't sleep that night. Would our son make friends? Would he ever wash his underpants? Would he wake up for his first lecture? The following day, he rang home. His voice was bright and there was no sign of the previous day's mood. Yes, he'd had a great night. He'd teamed up with the son of the parents on the steps and met some girls. They'd all skipped the welcome lecture and toured the pubs instead. No, he hadn't bothered with breakfast but stop fussing mum.

At the time of writing, he's now about to start his third year and our next child down is about to start her first at a different uni. But although he says it's been the best time of his life, we've had our teething problems which we've worked out for ourselves or with other parents going through the same thing. When researching the book, I constantly came across parents of older students who said they wished they'd had a book like this to help them. There are, after all, plenty of books on the market for the students themselves – but none for the parents left at home in the dark.

We hope our experiences (and those of the parents I interviewed) help you and your student kids to make the best of what really is a fantastic stage in their lives – and yours.

"Can you take a degree course in filling out UCAS forms?"

CHAPTER ONE

Idiot parents' guide to applying to uni

The good news is that at the time of going to press, universities still exist, despite all the palaver over fees. The bad news is that they have changed since your day. So even if you went to uni yourself, be prepared for some big developments (not all of which are good) when it comes to filling in the university application form.

For a start, it's called a UCAS form instead of the UCCA which existed in our day. (To preserve parental street cred, you have to pronounce that to rhyme with 'you' at the beginning instead of 'uck'.)

Secondly, any cool parent worth their salt never calls a university by its full name. It's known as a uni – even if in your day it was a common or garden poly.

Thirdly, you (because it's you that will be filling in the form since your child is still only semi-literate judging from his recent Key Stage results), no longer list the unis in order of preference. This is meant to stop certain unis from getting in a humph because they're not number one. Instead, you simply list six unis in random order – or you can put fewer than six if you don't fancy the full quota.

Finally (not really but we don't want to swamp you all at once), paper applications on good old fashioned forms are disappearing. You might find your child's school dishes them out at the beginning of September but the likelihood is that most schools will encourage their students to apply online. UCAS is pushing this one although some students will say that online applications can take longer to do, particularly if you can't fit the text into the box. It is also – for those of us who prefer the paper age – a bit like sending a rocket into space. You press the Send button and hope it gets there. Somehow, it's much more reassuring to drop a form into a postbox, providing the postman doesn't keep it at his home for the next five years.

TIP

During the preceding summer term and the holidays, your child can download a sample application form so they know what's coming. Log onto the following:
www.ucas.ac.uk/getting/apply05/sample05.pdf. If you don't have acrobat, you can download it from **www.adobe.com**.

NARROWING IT DOWN TO SIX CHOICES

That's the easy bit. The tough part is selecting those six unis out of a possible 320 unis and colleges in the UK. In our day, you often didn't visit the university until you had an interview. Now, any diligent parent will either accompany or despatch their future student on a round of gruelling uni open days so they can check they like the atmosphere. In theory, this sounds sensible. After all, how else can you see that York actually resembles an NHS hospital unless you go there yourself?

On the other hand, thanks to the new A-level system which means there isn't a spare moment in the day for your kid to visit the loo, let alone a uni, there's not much time for the luxury of open days. Since you apply in the September of the preceding entrance year, it makes sense to go to the open days that are held in the previous summer, in other words 14 months before they start at uni. But that's during AS levels (the equivalent of our lower sixth) and they'll be swotting madly for modules. Our advice is to visit as soon after GCSEs as possible when there's a slight lull before the storm.

COURSE OR LOCATION?

Schools will tell you that the course is the most important thing to consider. Students will tell you that the location is possibly more vital. Our advice is to start off with the course (there are a staggering 50,000 to choose from) and narrow the opportunities down to as many locations as you can bear to visit.

But which course?

If your student has never had a burning urge to read Maths/Marine Biology/Chinese or another obvious subject choice, you've got a bit of fun in front of you. Obviously, it's tricky if your future student wants to read something that he/she hasn't done the relevant A levels for, so start with what he *can* do.

Log onto the UCAS website and find the Course Search. (Go to Student to Courses to Course Search.) This will give you the uni entry requirements and (sometimes) also an Entry Profile which has more detailed information on the course and selection criteria. Use the information to request a prospectus either online or using that old fashioned gadget, the telephone. A prospectus is much handier than merely having the info online. There's something rather comforting about being able to curl up on the floor with a glossy prospectus with proper pictures instead of getting eye strain from the screen.

Serious parents also fork out for books like the Times Best University Guide which lists unis in order of excellence, depending on the subject. Rather like school league tables, these can be useful but it's more important to find a course and uni that's right for your child instead of one that you can boast about because it came top in Oriental Studies.

Also check out the careers adviser at school and the local Connexions office (the local education authority will give you the number). Connexions is a government body which provides education advice. In other words, it's a new word for the Careers Office in our day.

TIP

As a taster, go to what is known as an 'Education Convention' organised by UCAS throughout the UK at different times and locations. This is a sort of university fair where several unis sell themselves and you can ask the right questions. Details on the UCAS site. **www.ucas.ac.uk/getting/events/index.html**

WE'RE ALL GOING ON AN OPEN DAY

Before your son definitely decides that Engineering at Lancaster is just the ticket, it's essential to go on an open day or visit the place first. Open days are useful because the staff are generally there to answer questions – and if they can't, you know the uni probably isn't for you. Dates for open days are usually listed under the unis on the UCAS website.

If you can't make the open day, try to go during term time rather than holiday when you get more of a flavour of the place. We visited Warwick in the summer when most self-respecting students were mid deep in the Amazon. Consequently, it resembled a concrete ghost town and our daughter was not impressed.

Be prepared to fork out on petrol/energy/days off work to tour the country on your quest for the Ideal University. Some schools organise their own jaunts and many students go with friends. This is fine except that sometimes it's useful to have an adult sounding board (especially if that adult also takes them to the pub for a break).

Try to encourage your inflexible teenager not to limit himself. He might think he doesn't want to go to a campus university because he wants to be in the centre of a town. But campus unis vary. He needs to see more than one to make up his mind.

CHAPTER TWO

Filling in the forms

Warning: This can seriously damage your health

Start nagging during the summer holidays if your future student is applying to Oxford or Cambridge. If he's not, the deadline is early January although it's sensible to apply by early October as unis start whittling down their applications by then. If your child intends to have a gap year, he can still apply now but put a different entry date (known as deferred entry).

Many unis don't call students up for interviews now (with the exception of certain subjects such as medicine). They make their choice based on the form, which is why the wretched thing is so important.

One of the most vital bits in the form is the Personal Statement – a section that has kept many a parent awake at night, thrashing with self doubts. The Personal Statement is your child's chance to say why the university should take her/why she wants to study Advanced Electronics with Oriental Studies/what she can give back to the uni in return. She also needs to say what she's done with her life so far that makes her a perfect candidate for the course.

If you're reading this some months before applying, pack your child off on a charity walk to the Himalayas now or think of some other equally impressive feat that will make your offspring's Personal Statement stand out amongst the tide of other forms. Even holiday jobs should go on this form if they prove that your son has used his initiative and got out of bed during the previous summer.

It's a well known but little discussed fact that parents write these Personal Statements – but beware. Don't let the rush go to your head. I know one mother who encouraged her son to say he'd interviewed World War I veterans who joined up in their thirties. At his interview at Oxford the history tutor pointed out that, according to the dates the boy was giving him, these veterans must be around 105.

TIP

Don't allow your child to fill in the form until he's logged on to **www.ucas.ac/uk/getting/apply05**. This gives down to earth advice on how to fill in the form and advice on the Personal Statement. For example, it suggests you say "what interests you about your chosen subject. Include details of what you have read about the subject." Also "What career plans you have for when you complete your course" and "Any job, work experience, placement or voluntary work you have done, particularly if it is relevant to your subject."

So get cracking with that Gold Duke of Edinburgh...

The same site has a Microsoft Word template for the Personal Statement so, in theory, you should be able to type it into the relevant space. Despite this, it took two hours for one boy of my acquaintance to do this – even though he had assistance from the headmaster.

What every parent should know *before* their child goes to university

Don't fall into clichés. Don't encourage your child to write 'I have always wanted to study history from the age of five' because unis get that all the time. Think of a way to make that passion for history stand out. For example, 'I want to know how people thought and what they believed in during the 12th century.'

Be truthful. They'll probably get caught out if they tell a whopper.

Do listen to the school's advice. Most schools look over the Personal Statement and they've had years of experience in knowing what will wash and what won't.

If you're unimpressed with the above, talk to a friend whose child is at a different school. They might have more useful handouts on what to put and what not to put on the form.

Say something catching in the Personal Statement which isn't necessarily academically oriented. For example, our daughter wrote that she was able to stand on her own two feet and take part in lively discussions because she had an older and a younger brother. I can vouch for that one.

Get your child to word that Personal Statement so it fits the criteria demanded by all the unis. If he's applying to read History at York and Philosophy at Manchester, his Personal Statement needs to be applicable to both.

Check your child's GCSE grades are high enough. Some courses demand a minimum grade in certain subjects.

Here's an obvious point that you might not know: your offspring, however talented, cannot apply to both Oxford *and* Cambridge.

And another point: it costs to send in a UCAS form. At the time of writing, it's £15 but the government might have other ideas...

Keep a note (or several) of your child's personal UCAS number.

It's essential to quote it in future correspondence with unis and to check their online progress to see if a uni has made an offer.

GOOD BOOKS TO HELP YOU FIND THE RIGHT COURSE/UNI

We have listed useful books and resources on the website to help you. You'll find the list at **www.whiteladderpress.com** alongside the information for this book. Posting it on the website means we can keep it regularly updated. Please let us know if you think anything should be added or amended.

CHAPTER THREE

When will you know if they've got a place?

The sooner you apply, the sooner the offers start coming in. Unis don't wait until that January deadline so your child might well get an offer by the end of October or early November. Oxford and Cambridge will call your student son/daughter for interviews in late November/early December and then let them know the result around Christmas (just what you needed).

Unis usually send an offer letter and this is followed by the official notification from UCAS that your child has a place. Your child can also check online (faster than the post) to see if they've been accepted or rejected.

Once they have had an offer, you don't need to get your child to do anything. Instead, you wait until you've heard from all six. UCAS will then send out a Statement of Decisions letter which gives a deadline for choosing the final two. (The dates vary from year to year, but it's usually in April.)

These are known as the Firm Choice and the Insurance. That's providing he's *got* two offers. If he hasn't got any, he needs to contact UCAS for details of its UCAS Extra scheme which allows him to apply for another course, usually between mid March and the end of June. If he's not successful with this, he can go through Clearing in September (see section on Clearing).

Before your student signs his name on the dotted line, he needs to know that the Firm Choice means he has to accept this if he gets the grades that the uni has asked for. The Insurance uni is usually one that has offered lower grades that your son would accept if he didn't do well enough for his first choice.

PERSONAL STORY

"Our daughter only had to get three Cs from Southampton as her first choice but she still decided to choose York university as her Insurance, even though its offer was three Bs. She knew she'd definitely get three Cs but she preferred York over the other insurances. In the end, she got three Cs but decided she really wanted York so she retook an A level. Her new grades were good enough for her to go to York a year later." *Mother of a first year student*

TIP

"Don't encourage your children to go online at night to check if they've been accepted or rejected. Bad news is usually easier to cope with in the morning when you're both less tired."
Father of a first year at Bournemouth

Still confused? Contact the UCAS Enquiries team on 0870 1122211

AFTER MAKING THE FIRM CHOICE

Don't think this is where you can sit back while your child gets on swatting for A levels and trying to get the required grades. Not a bit of it. As well as holding down a full time job/running the family/nabbing the occasional night of sleep, you need to look out for the following:

Accommodation form

This might seem premature but unis like to get organised in advance because there's not always enough bed space to go round. And although your teenager might like the idea of sharing a bed with a stranger, it might interfere with his studies.

So look out for the accommodation form which generally arrives in the Offer Pack that's sent by the uni when your child has got a place. Some unis don't send the forms then but wait until your child has accepted them as a Firm or Insurance uni.

It's essential that you fill in this form – with your student – before the cut off date or your child may not get accommodation. My daughter never received this form from one university (which we won't name) and we had to appeal to get a room. In the event, she didn't need it as the uni concerned was her Insurance – but it was a scary time.

Some universities guarantee hall spaces for those who put them down as first choice. Clever tactic on their part but not so hot if your offspring put them as number two. Most forms will ask if the future student is prepared to share a room (this doesn't mean he can request a fit female for a room mate). Fax the form as well as posting. The rush for rooms makes the first day of the sales look civilised.

You may not have a choice in halls but if you do, ask the following questions:

- How far is the hall from the campus?

- Is it self-catering or are meals provided? The latter is handy if your A grade offspring can only operate a tin opener.
- Is it single sex or mixed? (Does he want to be a monk?)

So he doesn't want to go into hall? Get him to think again. Starting off student life in one room – even if it is in a house full of students – can be lonely and difficult if your son doesn't get on with his flatmates. At least in hall he has a variety of friends to choose from and there will also be regular entertainment and meals provided.

Financial form

Take a deep breath. This is where it gets really complex. Even though you don't know where your son/daughter is going at this stage, you still need to apply for a financial form for the grant.

You can get one either online through **www.studentfinancedirect.co.uk** or by ringing your local education authority. This form is so complex that you require a Masters to fill it in. It's probably designed to put people off applying in the first place to cut down on the admin. Basically, it's a bit like a tax return where you have to put in your income and so on in order to see which financial benefits your child qualifies for. If in doubt (and believe me, you *will* be) ring the local education authority and get someone to talk you through it.

You still need to fill this in, even if you don't want to be means tested for a grant towards the tuition/hall fees. Those lucky parents who don't actually need a grant at all, often still take out the grant because it's interest free, and then invest it to get more interest.

This chapter is merely designed to alert you to the existence of this horrid huge form. Details of how much you're entitled to, and what this degree is actually going to cost you in hard cash, are laid out in Chapter Eight. But have a stiff drink before you read it.

TIME SCALE SUMMARY

First year of A levels Visit as many unis as you can. Check the UCAS website for details of open days. Get your student to do as many worthy things as possible in preparation for the personal statement.

Second year of A levels Nag them into filling in the UCAS application form as early as possible. The closing date is in January (the actual date will vary) or October for medical schools and Oxford/Cambridge. But universities start selecting from October onwards.

By March/April of the second year of A levels They should know which unis have accepted/rejected them. That's when they need to make a firm commitment to one and select a second as insurance. Also contact your local education authority for a grant/loan form. Fill in the accommodation form.

CHAPTER FOUR

So the results weren't great...

Your son has got his offer but it's dependent on certain grades. He's – somehow – got through his A levels without freaking out/walking out/not turning up. He's celebrated the end of exams in style and you've scraped up the evidence from his bedroom carpet. He's spent the summer in an African swamp/working at Tesco/driving you mad. Now all you have to do is wait for the results of his A levels which will determine which, if any, uni he's going to. Wasn't it easier when he was little?

There's nothing more nerve wracking than waiting for your child to open that envelope that tells them their A level grades. (Apart, perhaps, from waiting for the results of that pregnancy test 18 years earlier.)

If your child has a conditional offer and the results match the offer, they are guaranteed a place. You don't need to do anything apart from scream/open the champagne until UCAS sends an AS12 letter. You must then wake your child up from its celebratory stupor so it can return the reply slip with the letter within 14 days.

That's the good news. If your child's grades *don't* match the offer, resist the temptation to point out that if they had worked harder, life would be different. Be positive. They need you to be there for them so hide your feelings and get cracking on positive action instead of hitting the panic button.

First step is to get on the phone and ring the admissions department of the university concerned. Many universities will only talk to the student and not the parents so it's essential that you have already dragged back your offspring from whichever African swamp they've been spending the summer in.

"Some universities will still accept students even if their A level grades are lower than the offer," said a spokesman from Aimhigher, the government body to advise on higher education. "It depends on the course and other students' grades. Ask to speak to an admissions tutor and have your UCAS candidate number handy to quote in all discussions. If General Studies was not part of the original offer, it may be useful to mention this if you have done well. Remember that many unis have invested a lot of time in you before making the Firm/Insurance offers and they might well prefer you to a stranger taken from the Clearing System."

Right – so it's worth trying a bit of pleading, begging and cajoling (but resist the temptation to offer bribes even if you *do* own a pad in Florida and are willing to lend it to the uni staff in return for a small favour).

If that doesn't work, all is not lost. It's worth reminding your teenager of this as he thrashes around on the carpet, in a manner reminiscent of earlier toddler tantrums. His grades may be good enough to get into his second choice uni. Now he may say he doesn't want it and that he only wanted the first. Resist the temptation to say he's blown it because he didn't work hard enough/blew it during exams. Instead, gently point out the plusses of the alternative uni. Try to pinpoint features that actually make it more attractive than the other (further away from home/close proximimity to HMV/favourable ratios of whichever sex your child prefers).

If the grades aren't good enough for either first or second choice, there's still no need to send your offspring back to that African swamp. Soon after the results come out, UCAS will send you a Clearing Entry Form, known as a CEF with instructions on how the clearing process works. Clearing is the term for finding a place on a course that isn't yet full and which your son or daughter likes.

But you don't have to wait for that form. Log onto to **www.aimhigher.ac.uk** and search for Clearing. This will help you log on to the UCAS website which will list course vacancies. Certain newspapers like The Independent and The Mirror should also list university vacancies. Also call the Student One Life Helpline which is free during Clearing 0800 100 800.

Try not to panic or your child will do the same (and at this point, he *will* be a child rather than an 18 year old). Help them find a course they like and suggest they use this as an opportunity to consider subjects they might have dismissed before but might now find more appealing.

Having found a course, make sure your son/daughter has the right number of points. This might sound like a board game at this stage, and indeed the rules are similar. You need to hop across the right number of squares to win the prize. Then telephone the university you've found and see if there are still places left.

"You can phone as many places as you want but you can only send your Clearing Passport Number to one institution at a time," warns Aimhigher. "So make sure that when you eventually commit yourself through Clearing, you have chosen a course that you really want in a geographical location that you would be prepared to live in for at least three years." (More if they have to retake a year but let's not discuss that at this stage…)

WARNING: A-level students who have applied to read Medicine and don't get their grades can't usually retake to read Medicine again. This is, however, at the discretion of the uni so it's still worth making a phone call.

TIP

If you (or rather your disorganised offspring) lose that vital Clearing Entry Form, contact UCAS Enquiries on 0870 1122211, quoting your application number, and they can reissue one. You are only allowed one Clearing Entry Form, so if the missing one turns up, you must destroy it.

You/your student can also get confirmation of their uni place on exam day, by logging on to the UCAS website and keying in their personal number.

For hand holding and practical advice during this emotional time, ring The Student One Life Helpline on 0808 100 80000.

CHANGES TO THE SYSTEM?

There was great excitement in autumn 2004 when *The Times* announced that both predicted places and Clearing were going to be abolished, and that students would be able to apply for uni places only *after* they knew their results. Fantastic idea – anything to save those horrendous post A level mood swings, caused by fear of an uncertain future.

But then we discovered that no one has a firm date for when this might happen. Even so, the government has backed the idea (which has the fancy name of Post-Qualification Applications or PQA). So if you've got kids still at school, you can only hope their lives might be a bit easier in the future. From a practical point of view, this means taking A levels earlier, or first year students starting term later. And you thought you'd got shot of them...

LAST MINUTE ENTRY?

What if your son has spent his entire academic career swearing he doesn't want to go to uni – and now decides that actually, maybe he wouldn't mind after all...

Apart from delivering the I-told-you-so speech, you could push him in the direction of the computer and get a UCAS application form online from the UCAS website – log on to UCAS Application Requests. Alternatively, nip down to the local careers office. "Complete all sections of the form, except Section 3, and return the form to UCAS with the fee" says Aimhigher. "The form will take about two weeks to process and UCAS will then send you a Clearing Entry Form."

With any luck, enough students will still be dragging their heels in that African swamp for there to be some places left in Clearing.

TIP

"Remember that universities are there to help you and that when they advertise courses through Clearing, they need to fill their places," says Aimhigher. "So shop around and do not panic by taking a course that you would not have otherwise considered."

WHEN IS IT TOO LATE?

UCAS will process application forms received up to mid September. But even after that, it's not too late (just extremely tight). You can contact the universities or colleges direct.

*"I don't know why they call it clearing.
The process couldn't be foggier if you ask me..."*

CHAPTER FIVE

What if they've changed their mind about the course? (and other hassles)

Tough. Seriously, your dithering offspring needs to write to the university concerned, providing she hasn't changed her mind about the uni too. If she has, UCAS can't normally change the choice of unis after accepting the form, unless for exceptional reasons such as a change in family circumstances or other personal problems. If that's the case, ask the school to write to UCAS, explaining the situation and recommending that your child is allowed to change. However, this has to take place well before the results are out.

If it's after the results, and your child doesn't want to go to her Firm Choice, she needs to write to the uni concerned and ask to be released (a bit like an old fashioned engagement). If she doesn't fancy the Insurance uni either, she'd have to do the same. Then she could either go through clearing or reapply next year. Just what you wanted to hear....

THEY STILL WANT TO GO – BUT NOT QUITE YET

If your child has got his place but has suddenly decided he wants that year out after all, he (or you) needs to contact the university direct and see if they'll allow this. Good luck.

THEY'VE EXCELLED THEIR (AND YOUR) EXPECTATIONS

Well, miracles *do* happen. If they've got better grades than the school/they/you expected, they might feel they're too good for the uni they chose in the first place. That's the good news. The bad is that as they made a firm commitment by accepting the first uni, they have to contact the uni/college concerned to discuss their reasons for turning down their offer. It's then up to them to decide if they will release you from the commitment.

The same applies if they suddenly wish they'd chosen their Insurance university as Choice Number One (the Firm one). But in this case, they also need to check that the Insurance uni will accept them too as they might not be expecting them in view of the high grades. Don't turn down the Firm uni before you know your Insurance will take you. But the Insurance won't accept you until you're released from your commitment by the Firm uni.

AND IF THE WORST COMES TO THE WORST

You can always go through this with them again next year, and reapply through UCAS. Look on the bright side. You'll be a veteran and know what to expect (well, that might be exaggerating but you'll have some idea). And in the meantime, you could help them find some interesting gap work that will increase their experience so when they start uni, they'll be older and wiser.

WHAT IF THEY NEED TO RETAKE EXAMS TO GET BETTER GRADES AND REAPPLY NEXT YEAR?

Talk to the school. After all, they need to take some responsibility too. The school might suggest your child retakes certain modules. Some schools help former pupils do this during the autumn term with extra lessons or by allowing them to attend classes with the year below.

Your 18 year old might find it demeaning to sit with the babies but there are other ways. Check out local colleges to see if they run retake courses. If you have enough dosh, consider a personal tutor. Log on to **www.tutors.co.uk**, an organisation which is recommended to parents by many schools.

FIX! THEY DIDN'T MARK IT RIGHT

If the results are way out and you wonder if a paper has been marked correctly, contact the school immediately. The school can request your child's exam papers and then judge whether, in the teacher's opinion, it should be remarked. If you/the school still aren't happy, the school can appeal to the awarding body and the Examinations Appeals Board which is independent. This can take time so contact the university your child hoped to go to and explain the school is launching an appeal.

I WASN'T WELL!

Let's hope you're reading this bit before the results come out. If your child was ill or the cat died or mum left home round about exam time, someone needs to write to the examining board immediately after the exam. Don't wait until after the results are out or it looks like an excuse.

CHAPTER SIX

At last they're off your hands. Or are they?

You've spent all summer coping with your post A level moody teenager. You've lent him the car. You've forked out for that backpacking trip. And you've tried to reassure him when he panics in case he hasn't got the grades and is destined for a career stacking shelves.

But now the A level results are out. He knows where he's going – or not going. Suddenly, you're about to lose your 'baby'. And on top of all the emotional angst, you've got to get him back from the pub/supermarket job/backpacking trip round Europe, and help prepare him for the next adventure: University.

Naturally, he'll be cool. All he needs is a pair of jeans and your cheque book. Besides, he's got another month before he goes. What's the rush? In fact, the end of August and the beginning of September is the period when everything starts to happen. As soon as he signs on the dotted line of the UCAS form, confirming his acceptance of that university place, your postal address will be deluged with letters from the uni, the accommodation office, the students' union and any other organisation remotely connected with the seat of learning he has chosen.

THEY'VE FORGOTTEN WHERE THEY APPLIED – OR WHY

OK, they remember the name of the place but they saw it during a week of cramming in other unis as well and they can't really remember specifics, like how many bars there are.

Don't worry, unis make allowance for this. Many have information days which are held for students who already hold offers. If you didn't get to one of these, ring the uni and see if there are any during the summer before your child actually packs his case.

Alternatively, you could just take your almost-student off on a day jaunt to visit their future seat of learning. But go at a time when there are other students around, ideally before the end of the summer term. Otherwise, you'll be visiting a shell with only a few saddos who've chosen to stay on in the holidays. And the chances are that your offspring won't fancy that uni any more and bail out altogether…

Still, that would save on the fees, wouldn't it? (Only joking.)

FILE EVERYTHING

Look out for the post. Don't allow your son to 'file' any of the above literature into the bottom drawer of his desk or lose it in the bowels of his bedroom alongside last month's festering bowl of cereal. Keep all relevant information in a see-through envelope and put it in your own desk. Take photocopies so you have a spare when he loses the originals.

TIP

Encourage your son/daughter to organise himself too, says a spokesman for the student support service at St Andrews. ' They should know how much their grant is and who to contact if it does-n't arrive. If you do it all for them, they won't learn.'

ACCOMMODATION

If you filled out an accommodation form earlier in the year, you should get confirmation and details of your student's pad as soon as you've confirmed your place. If not, get on that phone fast. Unless you want to fork out an annual season ticket for a B&B.

"Mum, which uni am I going to? Was it Durham or Dublin?"

CHAPTER SEVEN

Special needs students

The Special Educational Needs & Disability Act (2001) makes it unlawful for institutions to discriminate against disabled students in how they admit students and the services they provide.

However, universities do vary in their facilities and you will probably have gone into that when applying. But now it's nearly time to go, you might need to check up on some points. The first point of call is the Student Support Service – every uni has one. (Perhaps we should launch a Parent Support Service too.)

Check out what facilities there are if your son/daughter is deaf/blind/uses a wheelchair etc. These vary. Bristol University, for example, is one of many that provides an electronic note taking service. Someone from the uni types the lecture onto a laptop and this is linked to the student laptop so it comes up on the screen.

Also check there's transport from hall to lectures. And see if they can put you in touch with other students in the same boat if you have specific questions. Some unis allow students to take specially trained dogs. Some also provide helpers. If not, contact your local social services and/or education authority.

Also talk to Skill, The National Bureau for Students with

Disabilities. **www.skill.org.uk** Tel 0800 3285050 **info@skill.org.uk**

Skill will also tell you more about the Disabled Students Allowance (DSA) which is designed to pay for the extra cost of a course due to a disability. This covers three areas:

- Specialist equipment allowance.
- Non-medical helper's allowance.
- General allowance for miscellaneous expenditure.

DSA's do *not* depend on your family's income.

CHAPTER EIGHT

Money

Note: all figures are accurate at time of going to press. However, they could alter if there's a change of government/change of government heart/student-parent rebellion.

You knew there was a catch to all that studying. By now, you'll already have filled out his grant application form. (If not, ring the local education authority fast – or better still, pay them a visit as it might be quicker.)

Even if you've filled out the paperwork, you or he still needs to tell the Student Loans Company (which administers loans on behalf of the government) which uni he has picked and give bank details. Naturally, he'll be too busy celebrating to bother with all this, so guess who has to do it? The problem is that because he's an adult (even if he doesn't act like one), you've got to drag him with you to the bank or, at the least, get him to write his signature on the form for the loan. So wake him up fast.

The forms you need for this should automatically come in the post. If they don't, find those details you filed away earlier, and contact the Student Loans Company. Also check that there's a branch of the bank he usually uses in the town he's going to. He might need to swap allegiances.

TIP

Shop around for the bank offering the most freebies to students opening new accounts. They all fall over each other at this time of the year to offer free gifts which range from five year railcards to cut price takeaways.

HOW MUCH DO YOU HAVE TO COUGH UP?

Despite all the horror stories in the press about top up fees, don't assume you're about to become bankrupt. Here are the facts. Tuition fees are currently £1,150 a year but will go up to around £1,200 in September 2005 and a maximum of £3,000 by 2006. (The exception is Scotland – see further down.)

If your child is going to uni in 2005 and the family income is less than around £21,000, the government (bless it) will pay the tuition fees. This might sound generous but it's actually the accommodation/living costs that are the killer. More of that later.

If your family income is roughly between £21,000 and £31,000, you'll get some help from the government for tuition fees. The amount of help varies but about 60 per cent of students get a reduction. (All of which goes to prove that you shouldn't have worked so hard yourself at school because it just means you're penalised when it comes to state benefits. But don't tell your student that now or he might just call it a day.)

CHANGES IN 2005 AND 2006

However, if your child is going to uni in 2006 or later, you don't *have* to pay the tuition fees at all when they're at uni. Too good to be true? Of course it is. What it means instead, is that the cost of tuition fees is just added to the student loan which they then pay back later when they're working and earning over £15,000 a year. In other words, it's procrastination. Or to put it in a less fancy way, it's putting off for tomorrow what needn't be done today.

Example: From April 2005, a graduate earning £20,000 pays back £8.65 a week, no matter what they owe.

The bad news is that the tuition fees are going up to a maximum of £3,000 a year depending on which uni they choose. But unis and colleges who charge higher tuition fees should have more bursaries and grants for students from low income families. So before you dismiss a more expensive university, check what handouts it's prepared to part with.

For students starting in September 2005 there is extra help for those whose family income is less than around £21,000. For these students, the government will pay the tuition fees for the entire three years.

However, this will not be applicable for students starting in 2006 when, instead, there are new Higher Education grants for families on certain incomes, which don't have to be repaid. If the family income is £15,000 or less, you can get a maximum of £2,700.

At the time of going to press, the government has just announced that students who are having a gap year in 2005 are exempt from the increase in tuition fees for the length of their course provided they have formal acceptance from their uni by 1 August 2005. In other words, they can still have their gap year and then pay the original £1,200. But if they go straight from school to uni in 2006 they have to pay the full whack. Good excuse to bum round Europe.

Meanwhile, as Prince Charles has doubtless discovered, Scottish universities charge £1,200 tuition fees for students from England, Ireland and Wales during the first three years. But tuition is free for the fourth year. You may or may not know that Scottish degrees last four years – but the good news is that they come out with an MBA at the end and an even bigger beer paunch.

If you're Scottish and your offspring is going to a Scottish uni, the tuition is free but you'll still get clobbered for hall fees unless you keep them at home. (Is it really worth it?)

WHAT ELSE DO YOU HAVE TO PAY FOR, APART FROM TUITION FEES?

Well, your kid has got to eat and sleep somewhere. Hall is usually the best place for new students to start out because they get to meet other moody students. If they just go into a bedsit or a house with other students, they might not find like minded moody students to hang out with.

Money wise, halls usually represent good value for money providing the food is up to scratch. Hall fees vary according to the university but, as a rough guide, they're around £70-£90 a week which will include meals. If your son wants to rent a room, work on a budget of around £70-£80 plus food plus bills. That's probably not much more than you'd spend on him if he was at home. Just look at the phone bill to reassure yourself.

On top of that there's money for drink and entertaining. Don't underestimate this. The average student will drink about £15-£20 a night for at least four nights a week. And there's nothing you can do about it, short of refusing to top him up. (A shrewd move when his bank balance goes into the red.)

WHY GET A STUDENT LOAN INSTEAD OF ANOTHER KIND?

Student loans aren't mean to sting you, like some other loans we could mention (but have been advised not to by our legal department). Student loans do have an interest rate but it's linked to inflation. In other words, the money that you or your student repays at the end of the day (century?) is the same in real terms as the money that was originally borrowed. According to the government blurb, "This means that the Student Loans Company does not make any profit from the loans. A student loan, therefore, is likely to be the cheapest form of borrowing your child will probably ever take out."

At the time of going to press, the maximum amount of loan is £4,095 for students living away from home. It's £5,050 for students in London and living away from home. And £3,240 for students living at home. Seventy-five per cent of the maximum loan is available to all eligible students, regardless of any other income. Whether you can get any or all of the remaining 25 per cent depends on the student's income and that of his family.

As we've said earlier (but we'll say it again, just to reassure you), your child won't have to start repaying a student loan until they're earning more than £15,000 a year. And even then, they don't have to pay too much back every month. Back to the government blurb which says, "For example, if your child's first job as a graduate puts him or her on the average starting salary of approximately £18,000 a year (about £266 a week after tax), they would only have to repay £5.20 a week. That's about half the cost of a CD." (What we want to know is where the blurb writer gets his CDs from.)

OTHER HELP WITH FUNDING

There are other sources of funding help which you might be able to tap into:

- **Access to learning funds** Access to learning funds are available through your college or university and provide help for students from low income households who may need extra financial help for their course.

- **The National Health Service (NHS)** offers bursaries for first degree courses across a range of medicine related subjects, including nursing and midwifery.

- **Disabled Students Allowance (DSA)** There are also disability allowances available to help cover any extra costs with carers, equipment or travel. Students who normally live in England and Wales apply for DSAs through their LEA.

- **Scholarships** Scholarship Search UK has a database of all undergraduate scholarships on the website.

CHAPTER NINE

More money (if only...)

EXTRA FINANCIAL HELP

Your son/daughter can also apply for extra funding if they go on to study teaching or work in the NHS. So encourage them to change careers immediately.

You can also get sponsorships, scholarships and other financial awards. For example, there are grants called Opportunity Bursaries for people who might feel they can't afford to go to college/uni. The bursaries are worth £2,000 each and are paid over the three years of your course. Even better, they don't have to be paid back. The grants are given to people who live in certain areas so ask your child's school or college to see if you're eligible.

There are also specific scholarships for certain subjects. For example, Engineering students can apply for a National Engineering Scholarship. Contact Scholarship Search UK on **www.scholarship-search.org.uk**.

There are also Access and Hardship Funds which your student can apply for once at university or college. These are aimed at students who are having genuine financial problems and don't just need to go on another shopping trip.

There's also the Disabled Students' Allowance (DSA) to cover costs directly associated with a disability such as the cost of a non-medical helper or specialist equipment or travel. For more information, log on to **www.dfes.gov.uk/studentsupport** or ring the free Student Support number on 0800 587 8500.

THE GOOD NEWS

The good news is that the government has pledged to write off any outstanding student loan debt after 25 years. By then, the kids will probably have put you in a home so you'll be past caring. Besides, another government will probably have changed the law by then.

COME AGAIN?

By now, you're probably as confused as we are with all these figures flying around. That's because everyone's financial position is different and it's hard to tell you, individually, what you're going to need in terms of hard cash. To find out how much your own child is entitled to, call the Higher Education Information Line on 0800 731 9133 or ring your Local Education Authority (if you can get through).

You could also find more information about tuition fees, student loans and grants in a fancy government booklet called 'How to Get Financial Help as a Student'. You can get this by ringing 0800 731 9133 or logging on to **www.dfes.gov.uk/studentsupport**. But it won't tell you any more than we have. If it does, write and tell us. Here's what the DfES says about financial support (these figures were accurate at the time of going to press).

What every parent should know *before* their child goes to university

FINANCIAL SUPPORT FOR FULL TIME UK HIGHER EDUCATION STUDENTS STUDYING IN ENGLAND, SCOTLAND, WALES OR NORTHERN IRELAND

1 ENGLAND/SCOTLAND

Current System (04/05 Academic Year (AY))

English domiciled students: studying in England

Pay a fixed fee of £1,150, which has to be paid up front

Receive a means tested fee remission grant of £1,150, so the students from the poorest backgrounds don't pay the fee

Receive a maintenance loan. Amount varies depending where they are studying. There are three rates: at home; away from home; and away from home in London

Receive a new HE grant of up to £1,000, means tested, on top of the maintenance loan. About 30% of students will get the full grant

English domiciled students: studying in Scotland

Pay a fixed fee of £1,150, which has to be paid up front

Receive a means tested fee remission grant of £1,150, so the students from the poorest backgrounds don't pay the fee

For those means tested to contribute to their fees, have this contribution covered by the Scottish Executive in the final year (under the Quigley agreement)

Receive the same maintenance package, loans and grants, as for studying in England

Scottish domiciled students: studying in England

Pay a fixed fee of £1,150, which has to be paid up front

Receive a means tested fee remission grant of £1,150, so the students from the poorest backgrounds don't pay the fee

Receive a maintenance package of loans and grants as determined by the Scottish Executive

Scottish domiciled students: studying in Scotland

Pay no fees, because the Scottish Executive pays the fixed fee on their behalf (effectively a non-means tested grant for fees)

Pay the Scottish Graduate Endowment post graduation (03/04 figure is £2,092). Mature students, lone parents and disabled students do not pay the graduate endowment

Maintenance package of loans and grants as determined by the Scottish Executive

Proposed System (06/07 AY)

English domiciled students: studying in England

Pay a variable fee, between £0 and £3,000. Fee may be deferred by taking out a loan for fees

Receive a new maintenance grant of up to £2,700, means tested. About 30 per cent of students will get the full grant. Most of this will be on top of the maintenance loan, although some will be in substitution for loan[1]

Receive a maintenance loan. Amount varies depending where they are studying. There are three rates: at home; away from home; and away from home in London

No fee remission grant

---

[1] Early modelling suggests £850 of the grant would substitute for loan and the rest would be in addition to loan, although this figure will need to be confirmed nearer to the time.

What every parent should know *before* their child goes to university

English domiciled students: studying in Scotland

Pay the fee as charged by Scottish HEIs. Fee may be deferred by taking out a loan for fees

We intend to pay the same package of grants and loans as for English students studying in England. The Scottish Executive is currently considering options following the outcome of the third phase of its Higher Education review and we understand the Scottish Executive will be announcing its conclusions early in the summer. We will confirm the position for English students in Scotland in the light of those decisions

Scottish domiciled students: studying in England

The package will depend on decisions taken by Scottish Ministers. The Scottish Executive is currently considering options following the outcome of the third phase of its Higher Education review and we understand the Scottish Executive will be announcing its conclusions early in the summer.

Scottish domiciled students: studying in Scotland

No fundamental change proposed. Eligible students will still receive free tuition regardless of family income. Probable revision of bursary support with a view to increasing amount available and numbers supported

2 ENGLAND/WALES

Current System (04/05 AY)

English domiciled students: studying in England

Pay a fixed fee of £1,150, which has to be paid up front

Receive a means tested fee remission grant of £1,150, so the students from the poorest backgrounds don't pay the fee

Receive a maintenance loan. Amount varies depending where they are studying. There are three rates: at home; away from home; and away from home in London

Receive a new HE grant of £1,000, means tested, on top of the maintenance loan. About 30 per cent of students will get the full grant

English domiciled students: studying in Wales

Pay a fixed fee of £1,150, which has to be paid up front

Receive a means tested fee remission grant of £1,150, so the students from the poorest backgrounds don't pay the fee

Receive the same maintenance package, loans and grants, as for studying in England

Welsh domiciled students: studying in England

Largely as for English students studying in England except Welsh domiciles may also receive a means tested Assembly Learning Grant (ALG) of up to £1,500 to help with essential costs of study

New students from 04/05 who, had the HE grant not been introduced, would have received lower amounts of ALG (£450 or £750) will receive £1,000 HE Grant instead. Those who would have qualified for the full ALG will receive £1,000 HE Grant and a £500 ALG top up

Welsh domiciled students: studying in Wales

Largely as for English students studying in England except Welsh domiciles may also receive a means tested Assembly Learning Grant (ALG) of up to £1,500 to help with essential costs of study

New students from 04/05 who, had the HE grant not been introduced, would have received lower amounts of ALG (£450 or £750) will receive £1,000 HE Grant instead. Those who would have qualified for the full ALG will receive £1,000 HE Grant and a £500 ALG top up

Proposed System (06/07 AY)

English domiciled students: studying in England

Pay a variable fee, between £0 and £3,000. Fee may be deferred by taking out a loan for fees

Receive a new maintenance grant of up to £2,700, means tested. About 30 per cent of students will get the full grant. Most of this will be on top of the maintenance loan, although some will be in substitution for loan[2]

Receive a maintenance loan. Amount varies depending where they are studying. There are three rates: at home; away from home; and away from home in London

No fee remission grant

English domiciled students: studying in Wales

Pay the fixed fee as set by the Welsh Assembly. Assembly Ministers have announced their intention to continue with the current fixed fee, uprating for inflation as usual. Fee may be deferred by taking out a loan for fees

We will pay the same package of grants and loans as for English students studying in England

Welsh domiciled students: studying in England

As for English students studying in England. The Assembly ELL Minister has already announced that Welsh domiciles studying in England will receive a means tested maintenance grant of up to £2,700

Welsh domiciled students: studying in Wales

---

[2] Early modelling suggests £850 of the grant would substitute for loan and the rest would be in addition to loan, although this figure will need to be confirmed nearer to the time.

Same as for English students studying in Wales. Baroness Ashton announced in Committee the Assembly's intention to provide a means tested maintenance grant of up to £2,700 for Welsh domiciles studying in Wales, subject to repeal of section 26(5) of the HE Act 1998.

3 ENGLAND/NORTHERN IRELAND

Current System (04/05 AY)

English domiciled students: studying in England

Pay a fixed fee of £1,150, which has to be paid up front

Receive a means tested fee remission grant of £1,150, so the students from the poorest backgrounds don't pay the fee

Receive a maintenance loan. Amount varies depending where they are studying. There are three rates: at home; away from home; and away from home in London

Receive a new HE grant of £1,000, means tested, on top of the maintenance loan. About 30 per cent of students will get the full grant

English domiciled students: studying in Northern Ireland

Pay a fixed fee of £1,150, which has to be paid up front

Receive a means tested fee remission grant of £1,150, so the students from the poorest backgrounds don't pay the fee

Receive the same maintenance package, loans and grants, as for studying in England

Northern Ireland domiciled students: studying in England

Pay a fixed fee of £1,150, which has to be paid up front

Receive a means tested fee remission grant of £1,150, so the students from the poorest backgrounds don't pay the fee

What every parent should know *before* their child goes to university

Maintenance package made up of loans and bursary. Higher Education Bursaries of up to £2,000 are available to students from low income backgrounds. Where a student is in receipt of the full £2,000 bursary their student loan is reduced by £1,500. If the student is in receipt of less than the full £2,000 bursary then the maximum loan is reduced by the amount of bursary they receive

Northern Ireland domiciled students: studying in Northern Ireland

Pay a fixed fee of £1,150, which has to be paid up front

Receive a means tested fee remission grant of £1,150, so the students from the poorest backgrounds don't pay the fee

Maintenance package made up of loans and bursary. Higher Education Bursaries of up to £2,000 are available to students from low income backgrounds. Where a student is in receipt of the full £2,000 bursary their student loan is reduced by £1,500. If the student is in receipt of less than the full £2,000 bursary then the maximum loan is reduced by the amount of bursary they receive

Proposed System (06/07 AY)

English domiciled students: studying in England

Pay a variable fee, between £0 and £3,000. Fee may be deferred by taking out a loan for fees

Receive a new maintenance grant of up to £2,700, means tested. About 30 per cent of students will get the full grant. Most of this will be on top of the maintenance loan, although some will in substitution for loan[3]

Receive a maintenance loan. Amount varies depending where they are

[3] Early modelling suggests £850 of the grant would substitute for loan and the rest would be in addition to loan, although this figure will need to be confirmed nearer to the time.

studying. There are three rates: at home; away from home; and away from home in London

No fee remission grant

English domiciled students: studying in Northern Ireland

Pay the fee as charged by Northern Ireland HEIs.

Receive the same maintenance package, loans and grants, as for studying in England.

Northern Ireland is currently consulting on proposals to introduce fee deferral and variable fees. Our intention, subject to the outcome of that consultation, is to offer English students studying in Northern Ireland the same package as English students studying in England: a loan to cover their fees, and the same grant and loan support for living costs. We shall confirm the position once decisions have been announced following the consultation in Northern Ireland, expected later this year.

Northern Ireland domiciled students: studying in England

The package will depend on decisions taken in Northern Ireland following the current consultation

Northern Ireland domiciled students: studying in Northern Ireland

The package will depend on decisions taken in Northern Ireland following the current consultation

---

TEACH THEM HOW TO BUDGET

Until your offspring make it to uni, the only budgeting they've probably had to do is make sure their allowance/pocket money/weekend job at Tesco stretches as far as a pair of designer jeans and a round of bacardi and cokes.

Now you're sending them off with a blank chequebook to sample the delights of Being Away From Home. Terrifying isn't it?

Channel that fear and focus it by making them sit down for a budget lesson (even the Prime Minister has to have one). Remember how you helped him learn his tables? Now's the time to help him learn to manage those figures for real. Talk him through how much money he has for one term and how it has to last at least eight to 12 weeks, depending on the length of his semester. This is probably the most amount of money he has ever had in his account. And if he blows it, you'll both be in trouble. Encourage him to take out weekly amounts rather than injections of cash as and when he needs it. If he doesn't know how to use a credit card machine, help him do so before he goes.

TIP

Keep a note of all his personal numbers so when he's lost them, you've got them to hand. Write down his credit card number, his National Insurance Number, his student number and his bank account number. It's probably an invasion of the Data Protection Act but you're his parent, aren't you?

YOUR VERY OWN BUDGET TABLE (COURTESY OF MORE GOVERN-MENT BLURB FROM **www.aimhigher.ac.uk**)

This is a cost of living calculator. If you log on to the Aimhigher website it will do the calculations for you.

Follow the steps below to generate both a weekly and a termly balance based on your predicted income and expenditure. You may alter values, and recalculate totals as many times as you wish.

1 Enter your termly income

Enter details of your predicted termly income in the boxes below:

	Amount	Average
Parental contribution £		–
Student loan £		1,250
Holiday or part time job £		160
Other £		–

2 Enter your termly and weekly expenditure

Enter details of your expected termly expenditure in the boxes below.

	Amount	Average
Rent £		800
Books £		100
Clothes £		100
CDs £		20
Other £		15

Enter details of your predicted weekly expenditure in the boxes below.

	Amount	Average
Food £		20
Leisure £		35
Local travel £		10
Household bills £		20
Telephone £		8
Other £		8

3 Calculate balance

Enter the number of weeks in the term (average is 12), and then click 'Go' to calcuate your weekly/termly balance based on the figure you have entered above.

Number of weeks per term ⬚ weeks

4 Totals

The following totals have been calculated based on the figures for income and expenditure entered above

Termly income £ ⬚

Weekly expenditure £ ⬚

Termly expenditure £ ⬚

Total weekly balance £ ⬚

Total termly balance £ ⬚

© HEFCE 2004. This site has been created by HERO

MORE BUDGET TIPS FROM AIMHIGHER, THE GOVERNMENT BODY TO PROMOTE HIGHER EDUCATION

Believe it or not, looking after your money is one of the most important things you'll learn to do while you're at university or college. It's something you'll need for the rest of your life.

Before you start your course have a look at the **Aimhigher budget calculator**. It's easy to use and will give you a rough guide to what you may have to spend your money on at university or college, to help you manage your money. The figures used as an example are estimates only based on average costs. The cost of living will vary across the country and what you're studying may also affect your outgoings. It's a good idea to get in touch with the university or college you're hoping to study at. They can give you average rent (if you're going to be living away from home) and travel costs for the area. You can find contact details on the UCAS website or try online prospectuses.

Students based in England or Wales can work out their loan and/or grant entitlements using the online calculator at Student Support Direct.

A few clues to hassle free budgeting

- Know your weekly budget – work out how much you can afford to spend on items like food, clothes, going out – and stick to it as best you can.

- Keep a list of any standing orders or direct debits that you set up – your bank will give you a printout if you ask.

- If you know you're going to receive one or more lump sums, set up an instant access savings account so that you can earn some interest on the money until you need to spend it.

- Keep a note when you use your cashpoint – it's easy to forget those late night tenners and they quickly mount up.

- Go and see your bank manager if you run into problems.

You might find it helpful to visit **www.studentmoney.org** which provides a guide to organising and planning your student finances.

OTHER USEFUL WEBSITES

We have compiled a list of other websites which can help you with budgeting, which you'll find at **www.whiteladderpress.com** alongside the information about this book. Posting the list on the website means we can keep it updated.

CHAPTER TEN

Network and domestic advice (which they'll ignore)

Remember that first day of school when you left him in the playground, terrified that he wouldn't make any friends? He won't admit it but that's how he's feeling now. He's leaving all those mates from school and going to a place where he doesn't know anyone. So give him a helping hand.

Do you know anyone else's teenager who is at the same university or going at the same time? Ask around. Even a phone number for a friend of a friend can be reassuring. Talk to them and persuade your teenager to do the same. Get as much useful information as you can about the uni. When my son went to uni, I talked to a work contact, Michele Elliott, director of Kidscape, whose boys had also gone to the same uni. She was a fantastic rock and I will always be grateful to her for the reassurance she gave me. My son also spoke to her boys and even though he made his own friends when he got there, it helped that he had their mobile number.

HELP HIM TO PHONE HOME

The good news is that your phone bill will go down once he's left home for uni. The bad news is that he'll only ring you when he wants something, and not when you just want to talk to see if he's alright.

So set him up with a mobile phone if he's sad enough not have one already. He'll push for a contract phone because it saves him the hassle of buying pay as you go vouchers. But do your research first. Find out the best contract deal and check the network's performance in the area he's going to. Make your own deal too. If he spends more than a certain amount, he has to pay the excess. It's all part of budgeting. Or shall we just call it tough love?

TIME FOR A CRASH COURSE IN DOMESTICITY

So you thought you'd brought him up to be a modern, caring male? That means he can just about put his plate on top of the dishwasher. Now he's going to a place where he may well be catering for himself. So you've got four weeks to teach him how to cook, load the washing machine and fill the iron with water. Start off with basics (cheese on toast) and warn him not to leave a grill/iron on and other basic safety measures. Get him to make you a meal if you feel resilient. The most useful thing I've personally bought my son is one of those George Foreman grills. He can do almost anything on it (well, I hadn't thought of *that* one...).

TIPS ON HEALTHY EATING

Even if they're going to be catered for, in-hall, they still need a reminder about the five portions of fruit and veg a day. Otherwise, they could go mad on the chips and ketchup – and stay like that for the next three years (more if they get hooked on uni life).

Stress the importance of going to breakfast. Too many kids think it's cool to go without nowadays – and it would be just your luck for your student to fall in with a crowd of non-breakfast eaters. Tell them they need breakfast to start the day – even if they're going to spend the rest of it sleeping...

CHAPTER ELEVEN

Packing

I HAVEN'T GOT ANYTHING TO WEAR!

And you thought students only needed a couple of pairs of jeans
and t-shirts... The good news is that your future student teenager won't be nagging you for a clothes allowance every week or
month. The bad news is that she won't have saved up her summer
holiday money to get the clothes she needs before she goes.

Don't go mad. Two pairs of jeans might not be enough if she
can't work the washing machine but she won't need six pairs
either. Point out that she probably won't have the storage space
she might have at home. So if she takes too much, there won't be
anywhere to hang it. (If she was ever going to, that is.)

Encourage her to take a mixture of student casuals and the odd
outfit for more formal occasions. OK, so she won't be seen dead
in a dress (when were you born, Mum?). But many university
tutors and departments organise drinks parties/socials even if
your teenager is more used to clubbing. So a smart pair of jeans
won't go amiss.

My student daughter has a tendency to bare her navel, even when
she's not in the bath. Sneak in a couple of warm woolly jumpers
when she's not looking. She might just be cold enough to wear

them, later on. Choose the clothes according to the university's location. Cardiff can be very wet and East Anglia, windy. St Andrews can be freezing but also has a microclimate of its own which means many students wear shorts up to November.

BOOKS

Well she is going there to study, isn't she? Is there a department reading list, hidden in that information pack the university has sent? If so, order the books for her so she can take them up and be ready. If there isn't a list, you could try getting her to ring the department and ask for a list in advance. Second thoughts, she's right. They'll think she's a nerd. But do encourage her to pack her old A level notes and essays; it's surprising how much they come in handy. She might even be able to crib from old work.

ADDRESS BOOK

Does she know your office number? Does she know grandad's address so she can send him a birthday card? Buy a hardback notebook to copy down important information for her along with her student identity number, national health number, bank account number and other information at the back, in case she loses the originals. Also give her a diary so she can write down lectures and tutorials and so on. She won't use it but it will make you feel better.

FUNNY/RUDE POSTCARDS AND STAMPS

It might make her more inclined to keep in touch.

TIP

Remind your offspring to get photos done of themselves. These are often needed for student union cards and so on and it saves time and money (theirs, not yours) if they take them with them.

COMPUTER

Most universities expect students to bring their own computers. Laptops can be easily brought home at the end of term but they are also easy to pinch at university. Many students find it easier to work on big screen computers but they are a pain to bring home. We've personally chosen the latter. Stock her up with CDs or DVDs so she can save everything. Or she could email her work back to the computer at home. Check what the hall policy is on computer links and costs. Spread the cost by paying monthly installments or checking out the second hand section at your local computer store.

PERSONAL STORY

"We bought our daughter a computer instead of a laptop after a friend of hers – who had a laptop – went to the end of her corridor to make a cup of coffee, leaving her door unlocked. When she got back, her laptop had gone with all her work on it. She hadn't backed up on floppy discs and she never found the laptop." *Mother of a second year student at Southampton*

In his excellent book *The Insider's guide to **Getting A First** (or avoiding a Third)* Mark Black advises students to invest in computers and books if they can possibly afford it, in order to give them the best chance of success. Here's a summary of what he has to say:

"Invest financially to get a First, just as a football team provides facilities for its players. Buy fast PCs with full Microsoft Office suite. Computers can be less expensive if you have them made. Also invest in broadband internet access so you can download lecture notes from the university website in seconds.

"Get PowerPoint to make your presentations look professional. And invest in an all in one printer/scanner to print off lecture notes/copy other people's notes overnight and give them back the next day.

"Get your own copies of recommended books. The library is invariably out of stock when you need books the most. Read round the subject instead of just the books set out on the reading lists. Check out local bookstores and register with amazon.co.uk.

"Subscribe to independent sources of information which you can reference in your assignments. ft.com and economist.com are both good examples of this."

STEREO

Yes, she'll want to take it. So don't bother pointing out that you'll never fit it in the car. (See below.) Also buy her a clock/radio alarm so she gets up for lectures. Yes, we're only joking. No, all right, we're not.

TIP

Include a familiar duvet cover/bedspread/blanket/cushion to make them feel more at home. Preferably one which smells of the dog/one you wanted to get rid of anyway.

THE CAR
(taking it with them, that is, instead of merely travelling in it)

We're still rowing about that one in our family. Our view is that they might kill themselves/take our only spare vehicle/spend their grant on petrol/not get to know other people because they'll be in the car and others will be walking or cycling. They could also find themselves acting as an unpaid taxi driver to friends who will make so much noise that it will be hard for the driver – your child – to concentrate. Insurance companies also charge more for students taking a car to uni and even if you don't tell them, they have a sneaky way of finding out.

Their view is less complex. It's their car and even if it isn't, they want it.

Good luck with the negotiation. You might be saved by university rules since some universities, such as Cambridge, actively discourage students from bringing their own. If there's no getting out of it, check the insurance and make sure there's somewhere safe to park it at uni. You can always say 'I told you so' when they crash it or have it stolen.

TIP

Pack a door stop to wedge their door open in hall. It will encourage new friends to pop in. (You can also use it at night to keep intruders out.)

CHAPTER TWELVE

More essentials to sort out before they go

INSURANCE

Check the hall has insurance to cover your student's possessions. If you're lucky, your own household insurance might do it anyway. Insurance firms like Endsleigh specialise in student insurance. **www.endsleigh.co.uk**

LABEL EVERYTHING

And you thought you'd never have to sew on another school uniform label. By the time they've mislaid their jumpers (and more intimate items) of clothing in other people's rooms, they'll need more than a label to remember whose is whose – let alone who is who. But a label is a starter.

Get them to put their mark on CDs too, and stereos and laptops and anything else that might get borrowed or go walking. Someone is less likely to nick it if it bears a name.

TIP

Get boxes from supermarkets or companies like Yellow Boxes. See section on Websites at end.

HEALTH

Your student will be registered as a university patient which means that during holiday time, she will be seen as a 'temporary patient' by her own GP at home and will have to sign a form to confirm this. It's yet another tough reminder that although your daughter is home for the holidays (that's if she *is*), she's left home for good as far as the authorities are concerned.

As further proof, her notes will no longer be with the family GP but at university – tricky if she wants to check vaccinations and so on when she's home with you, as she'll then have to ring the uni medical centre instead for the info.

WARNING: If she's not around and has asked you to sort out her vaccination dates etc, the medical centre doesn't have to give you the vital information as she's over 18 and you might be snooping into other medical matters (heaven forbid).

TIP

If you can't remember which vaccinations your child has had up to the age of 18, ring the local health authority. They should give you the number of your local Child Health Centre which will have a record of all jabs and pricks from 0-18. After that age, you're on your own unless you're one of those organised mums that has a special Vaccination book and faithfully records every date.

Also have a pre-uni chat with your about-to-be-student. Yes of course she knows about the morning after pill (she could probably tell *you* more about that), but would she know what to do if she was stung by a bee? Pack a medical kit with basics like plasters, antihistamine cream, paracetamol and so on.

MEDICAL ESSENTIALS

Paracetamol (explain these shouldn't be taken with alcohol)

Thermometer

Plasters

Tablets for constipation

Tablets for an over active stomach

Sick bowl – extra

Antihistamine cream and tablets (for allergies/stings)

Condoms (for both sexes)

Flu capsules

Antiseptic cream

Nail scissors

Most universities run a new students appointment scheme during the first term, to give basic advice and sometimes checks. Encourage your student not to miss it. My son still hasn't made his and he's in his second year now.

GOOD WEBSITE

www.studenthealth.co.uk. Fascinating website with just the right irreverant/common sense attitude to health. For example, it contains facts such as the one below as well as free condom giveaways:

"Carbohydrates should provide around **50%** of your energy requirements and are therefore a very important part of your diet. Your total carbohydrate intake consists of two main subgroups – sugars and starches. You get sugars from fruit and vegetables and also from dairy products, honey, table sugar and confectionery."

"*Just remember you're always my little bubsie and I wuv you.*"

CHAPTER THIRTEEN

Getting there

Personally, I think it's tough for students to arrive on their own. Even if they insist they don't want you accompanying them as though they were starting school for the first time, they might feel differently when they're standing at Euston station with two suitcases in each hand, wondering which platform they should be on. By then, they'll probably be feeling rejected because you aren't with them – even though they banned you from coming. You can't win – but then again, what's new?

On the other hand, when you do go with them, you have to pretend you're not really there. You can chauffeur them, carry their cases in, hand over a wadge of dosh and then basically beat it. Whatever you do, never embarrass them by crying/sniffling/laughing loudly and declaring that the house will finally be peaceful now/handing over their vitamin pills/telling them to get an early night after the journey.

When our eldest son went to uni, I did two of the above (guess which). My husband was much more practical and knocked on the door of the student's room next to our son's. He introduced himself, introduced our son and suggested that the stranger might like to show our son round the bar that night. Amazingly, the unsuspecting neighbour took it in good humour (his own father had reacted in a similarly odd way when dropping him off in the first year) and introduced our son to everyone else on the corridor.

TIP

Remember that every other first year is feeling scared inside, however cool they seem on the outside. And if they're not, they're obviously too arrogant to be a good friend.

PERSONAL STORY

A friend's daughter, starting at Nottingham, was thrilled to find herself invited to her neighbour's room to share a large chocolate cake that the neighbour's mum had made. Everyone in the corridor was also invited to pile on calories and get to know the others. Now that's what I call a clever mum.

TRANSPORT

If you can, fit everything in the car. It's a darned sight easier than struggling on to a train with the contents of your son's bedroom in both hands. If you don't have a car or it's not big enough, consider hiring one – or even a van – for the day (you'd be amazed at how many parents do this).

That's the easy bit. Parking the car is something else that demands more than a degree. Ideally, do it the night before or you'll spend so long trying to get everything in/yelling at everyone who comes into close contact, that your new student will be late for registration. Try to clear a space for the driver to see out of the back window or you'll be stopped by the police before you get there.

Don't be alarmed when the car ends up looking like one of those line ups on the kind of quiz programme when you can keep what you remember. When we made that first journey, we couldn't even see our son in the back because he was camouflaged by stereos, duvet, pillows and suitcases. It was probably just as well because he was in a filthy mood all the way up to Scotland. I wasn't fooled – it was a fit of nerves. He wanted to leave us but it was also scary. So don't be offended by filthy behaviour during the journey. Just add your own for good measure.

If you can't fit all the luggage in the car, check out your local courier firm. Believe it or not, it's possible to courier a comput-er/suitcase/stereo for under £60. But check your insurance, especially if you have to pay the first £100 quid or so.

HELPING UNPACK

University accommodation can vary tremendously. Our son's room at hall was so tiny that it could barely fit in three people together with his bed, desk and wardrobe. If you really feel it's unsuitable, you could go down to the accommodation office and put his name on a waiting list for an alternative.

On the other hand, you'll be surprised at how fast he settles in once he's made friends. Accommodation offices are so used to horrified parents and students turning up their noses at the cubi-cles they're presented with, that they usually advise you – on the waiting list form – to think carefully before moving. A friend's son still went ahead but found that when he'd moved to another hall, with superior accommodation, he missed the mates he'd met during the first fortnight at the grotty hall. Now, two years later, he still socialises in the first hall and sleeps in the second.

What every parent should know *before* their child goes to university

It's not an ideal situation.

Some unis have decidedly superior accommodation. In fact, it might be worth checking out the rooms before the course. Nowadays, some halls even boast en-suites (so that's where your tax goes). And whatever you do, don't start acting prudish if your son/daughter ends up on a mixed corridor. It doesn't mean they're going to end up sharing a bath after a week. In fact, it probably means the opposite. There's nothing like using the loo/shower/washbasin after a member of the opposite sex has left behind their bodily hair, to put you off, well, sex – for life.

Whether your student has superior or inferior accommodation (with or without male hairs in the bathroom), it's nice to make it as much like home as possible. Doubtless he will have brought his posters, music and hopefully the odd book. A noticeboard is also nice to stick pictures on and maybe a whiteboard to write notes about lectures etc. I also brought a diary for my son so he could put in essential work deadline dates. To this day, it remains empty. What was more useful was his duvet (the smell reminded him of home) and coat hangers. We had a fantastic row about these when packing at home, as he insisted he wouldn't need them. Guess who was right?

Cleaning essentials might be useful too. A friend had to wipe the mildew off the wall of her daughter's hall bedroom in a prestigious university which I'd better not name.

I'd also packed some food extras like hot chocolate, soup and cereal, even though the hall was partly catered for. There wasn't room to fit it in so we ended up taking it home, along with the linen basket (a rubbish bag under the bed is just as good) and half his CD collection because there was nowhere to put it.

What you *do* need to pack is more cash. Yes, we know you've mortgaged yourself up to the hilt to put him through uni. But he'll need hard cash to get him through that first week. There'll be all kinds of unforeseen expenses like hall subs. Not to mention the odd pint or two at the union to get him used to these strange surroundings.

TIPS

- Get a bag of pound coins from the bank and leave them in his room for the laundry.

- Also buy a small wall planner for the wall. He can write down essay deadlines, end of term dates, birthdays and so on.

- Check if there's communal storage space for those big cardboard boxes that contained the stereo. If so, keep them for packing at the end of term.

SECURITY

Whatever you do, don't tell him in a loud voice to lock his door every time he goes out into the corridor/to the loo/kitchen. His neighbours will immediately think they're suspected crooks. Students don't lock their doors when they're not far away. It's not cool. But at the same time, things do get nicked sometimes.

The best thing is to help him find a safe place to keep essentials like bank card, passport, ID and so on. I gave my children a transparent envelope each (transparent so they would remember what was inside) and got them to hide it under their underwear in the wardrobe.

PERSONAL SAFETY

If you can, encourage your daughter to carry a rape alarm. Of course she'll think you're overreacting – until something happens. You can buy really tiny ones now so she can hide it and won't look like an idiot. Give her the usual chit-chat about not walking home on her own at night. You'll have done this before at home but it's worth pointing out that, sadly, bad things still happen to women (and men) at university too. Universities themselves are very aware of this and many run self-defence courses at the union.

Talk too about date rape and, even if she thinks she knows all about this kind of thing, spell out that it's more than OK to say No if she doesn't want sex. Talk too about drink spiking which is becoming increasingly common. We've said it before but we'll say it again. Never put down your drink in case someone pops something in it. And we're not talking straws here.

TIP

Print out personal home information like email contacts and put it in a plastic cover for his wallet/her handbag. It gives you the reassurance of knowing that someone *could* contact you if your student was in an accident.

CHECK OUT THE LOCALITY

Having unpacked and made the place less like Brixton prison, it's not a bad idea to check out the hall facilities. He probably won't want to come along with you but at least you can tell him where the laundry is. If he won't be seen in the corridor with you, he might not be averse to a quick recce round town to see where the station/HMV is.

> **TIP**
>
> Don't expect to drop your child at uni and run. Some unis expect parents to be around for the financial registration bit. That's when you have to hand over a cheque for tutorial fees and hall fees. Others arrange for you to do this by direct debit.

HANGING AROUND

Help him unpack but don't outstay your welcome. He doesn't want to be known as a wimp. This is a horrible time for you but somehow you have to be brave. Hold onto your tears until you get into the car. Remember too that although he's almost grown up, it's natural for you to be upset. On the other hand, there *are* plusses. You'll be able to get into the bathroom. You won't be yelling at him to come down for supper. Your phone bill will be halved. You'll have to talk to your partner. You have more time for the other kids.

If the university is a long way from home, you might need to stay the night. If so, try to do so the night before registration. Your student won't want you staying over on his first night when there will be lots of events for student fresher week. I mean, what can be more embarrassing than mum and dad turning up the following morning when the poor kid is recovering from his first real student hangover?

CHAPTER FOURTEEN

She's gone!

The worst bit is coming back to an empty bedroom which is still strewn with teenage cast offs and posters that would normally give you nightmares but which now seem sentimentally cute. Allow yourself to cry/jump for joy. Don't, under any circumstance, start to tidy up or you'll feel worse. Wait a few days until you feel more like yourself – and you will. Eventually.

The worst bit is the first two weeks. You'll wake up in the night in a cold sweat panicking about whether your daughter has made it back to her hall room safely after the first fresher disco. You'll be overtaken with panic and irrational fears. Did she take the rape alarm you insisted on buying her? Did she have too much to drink? Is she still out there somewhere? The only thing to do is go back to sleep. If there is a problem, you will know about it sooner or later. This sounds tough but what else can you do? Ring her hourly? Forget it. She won't answer the mobile.

As the days go by, you'll be surprised at how you adapt to her absence. You'll still miss her but the pain/relief gets more normal. Talk to friends and neighbours who've been through it. I was surprised by parents whom I'd always thought were tough but admitted that they too had been knocked sideways by their terrible teen's departure.

When they go away, don't fill their space with your clutter. Otherwise, they'll come back to find they haven't got anywhere to put their things.

The great thing about mobiles (we know about the downside) is that you can keep in touch, providing they've got theirs switched on. There's nothing wrong with ringing her the next day to see what she did last night. When she tells you (if she does), you'll wish you hadn't asked. However, it's not a great idea to ring every day from then onwards. She needs a chance to settle down and the sound of your anxious voice on the other end is more likely to unsettle her. When children go to boarding school, there's usually a rule that parents shouldn't ring for the first week or fortnight. Harsh as it sounds, there's a reason for that. They need time to get used to their new surroundings without someone making them feel homesick.

TIP

- As well as or instead of ringing, write a newsy letter or maybe just send a funny postcard. In today's electronic age, something on paper that can be read again instead of deleted, is a great comfort. An odd fiver slipped inside might be nice too.

- Don't ring too often eg every day on the hour. You need to give them a chance to settle – and you need to 'wean' yourself too.

- Learn to text. It's less intrusive than a phone call and it won't interrupt your son if he's in the middle of someone – sorry, something – else.

EFFECT ON OTHER CHILDREN

You can also distract yourself by concentrating on the other children at home, if you've got them. They'll be feeling pretty fed up too. Not only will you have ignored them for the past month in this heroic effort to get their elder sibling off to uni, but they will also miss their brother or sister – however much they loathed them when they were under one roof.

One thing that I hadn't thought of until our eldest went to uni, was the effect on family dynamics. If you've got three children, like us, it's likely that two of those three get on better. When one of those goes, they have to reassess their relationship. Maybe they'll start liking each other more. Or maybe less. Your unenviable job is to go along with this and try to keep the peace.

It's also weird having fewer children to juggle. For years, you've been complaining that it's all too much and you can't cope. Suddenly, you've got one fewer to wash for/cook for/moan at and it doesn't feel right. For some weeks, I still automatically laid the dinner table for five instead of four.

But don't panic. It's rather like the waking-up-in-the-night syndrome. You slowly get used to it. Or as Clare Rayner once told me during an interview, "everything passes, whether it's good or bad". As the weeks go by, you'll find yourself adjusting your focus and parenting style. Two kids instead of three? One instead of two? Fine. It gives you more time to spend on the remaining children.

For some weird reason, however, they don't always appreciate that. "I don't like being the only one at home," moaned one of them when the second was away on a school trip and the eldest at uni. So don't overdo it. Just because you've only got one, doesn't mean you have to watch their every move. Give them space.

What if the last one has left for uni? That's when you need to rediscover yourself and your partner, if you still have one. It's a big deal and one which needs space of its own. (See Chapter Twenty one.)

Meanwhile, you can help your other kids keep in touch with their older uni sibling. Even if they're not that keen, it's important if you want them to stay close in life. It's easy at this stage for them to drift apart because they're no longer under one roof. So encourage them to text/MSN on the computer or even write letters. Our youngest son missed his brother so much that he moved into his bedroom for comfort. This was, however, only temporary. During the holidays, he went back to his own room.

Don't, whatever you do, instantly give her room a makeover. When she comes back, she'll want to find everything is the same. I know someone who actually rented out their daughter's bedroom to a paying guest. After one term, that daughter never came home again. Well, do you blame her?

PERSONAL STORY

One friend of mine, fed up because her daughter rarely rang home, encouraged her to register with Yahoo and join in conversations with family and friends. It was less formal than a phone call and she learned all sorts of interesting titbits about her life that she might not have done from a text. "She would log on and see that we were 'talking'; so she'd just join in. She did it more often than if she'd had to make the effort and write a formal email to us."

CHAPTER FIFTEEN

Helping them through the first few weeks

They may not need this. After all, they've got their new friends and the union bar. What else could they want? But some kids – and that includes grown up ones – find it more difficult to make friends than others. And there's nothing worse than hearing your lonely student child at the other end of the phone, saying she still hasn't made friends and she's wondering if she's done the right thing by coming here.

This happened to Angela from London whose son went to Kent university. "The first week was the worst. I thought he'd be fine because the union had lots of events planned for fresher week. But he's always been a bit shy when it comes to making friends. To make it worse, he was in a corridor where none of the other students were first years. Because he had come up a week early for fresher week, he was the only student on the corridor."

Most halls are sympathetic enough to make sure there's more than one fresher in the same locality. But if your son finds himself in that situation, do something about it. Ring the warden – each hall has one – and see if he can be moved.

You can't force your offspring to go to social events during fresher week. In fact, most kids have to be dragged back from them by their new friends, quite the worse for wear. But you could point out forthcoming events when you see them advertised, either from the pile of literature you'll be inundated with before starting or at the union when you're looking around on the first day.

On the other hand, don't panic *too* much if you're not able to contact your student during fresher week. For those of you who didn't experience this particular delight youself, it's a non-stop array of parties and discos and whatever else your worst nightmares can think of. Most events are organised by the union but the hall committee will also have some tricks up its sleeve.

And if you're wondering what happened to Angela's son, you'll be glad to know there was a happy ending. "He didn't make proper friends until the end of the first term. For a few weeks, he even considered leaving but I persuaded him to stay on by reminding him that it took time to make friends at secondary school. Then he joined a climbing club that was advertised in the union and met people whom he really got on with. They're still his friends now he's in his third year."

REGISTRATION

Killjoy parents might be relieved to know that fresher week is not just all drink and sex. There's also the more serious matter of registration. Some unis have this on the first day so if your student really still needs you to hold his hand, you might like to hang around to make sure he actually gets round to filling in the right forms.

Many unis also require you to log on to the university computer system. This can be the most complex process you can imagine unless you're a computer geek. It normally requires several hours of queuing for the right password and then obtaining, through the university, the right technology to connect your laptop to the vast university network. At least, that was our experience. So allow a few hours if you want to be on hand. Or else just leave him to it and go home.

Don't leave, however, without checking his email address. (He might have decided to change it without telling you.) Also remind him – even though the uni blurb will have done this already – that tutors usually communicate with students through the university email address. So they *must check* them regularly and not just log on to their hotmail account that all their friends use.

It goes without saying that your student is going to need a computer point in their room. Most halls provide these automatically but if your student is not in hall, you need to sort this out with the landlord. To tide you over, the library will also have computers where your son can access those messages from his tutor, wanting to know why he didn't turn up for his first seminar. But you don't want to know about that, do you?

WHEN FRESHER WEEK IS OVER

This might be the time for a reminder phone call or email that work starts the next day. Has she got her files together? Has she checked out her timetable in the relevant faculty? Has she any idea where the right lecture theatre is?

TOP TEN TIPS FOR SURVIVING STUDENT LIFE
from Aimhigher

1 **The Student Union is your friend** – they will be able to provide support and offer many of the services and social activities available on campus.

2 **Make friends** – while university or college can be daunting at

first, remember that other students are in the same position as you. Uni often means moving away from home, parents and friends – so take advantage of the fact that other students are also looking to make friends.

3 **Have a social life** – you are at university to study, but it is also a fantastic opportunity to have fun. You are going to be there for a number of years; you want to make sure you don't burn out. It is important that you get some relaxation and enjoy yourself. Most university student unions have a variety of activities, clubs, societies and student bars. While you probably shouldn't be partying every night, it is important to have some time off.

4 **Take time to adapt** – university or college means that your life is going to be very different. For some people campus life takes some getting used to but don't forget it is meant to be a positive experience. It might take you a little while to get used to things being done differently but you'll get there.

5 **Find out where the library is and do the tour** – the library will be vital to your studies, it will provide many of the resources you'll need. Most campus libraries will offer a tour to new students – it may not sound exciting, but it can be an incredibly useful way of finding out what they offer and how to easily locate what you need.

6 **Manage your money** – for many, being a student means that you won't be rolling in money. But if you plan carefully and stick to a budget, you'll be able to enjoy yourself without ending up in too much debt.

7 **Manage your time** – the more organised you are, the less stressful studying will be. Plan ahead so that you don't have to stay up all night finishing an essay that is due the next day.

8 Get to know your new town – many people get to live in a new town or city when they start university or college. Get to know the area, what it has to offer, the best places to eat, the best clubs and bargain shopping.

9 Keep in touch with family and friends – make sure you keep in touch with family and friends back home. They will still be able to offer you support and encouragement.

10 If things go wrong – if anything in your life is going a bit pear shaped and it's affecting your studies, you should make sure that you tell your personal tutor or course director about it. They may be able to allow an extension on course work or take it into account when marking your exams. If they don't know – they can't help.

*"But Dad, it's awful here. If I just want a cup of tea
I have to make it for myself."*

CHAPTER SIXTEEN

Problems and how to cope

Sometimes, of course, they're *not* all right. He might not come
clean about these problems to begin with. So you need to smell
them out with that intuitive parental interfering streak that
you've been nurturing since they were small. You'll get further on
the phone as you can tell from the tone of their voice if something is up. Texts and emails don't always have the same feed-
back.

HOMESICKNESS

However desperate he was to get away from home, the truth is
that when he's in his tiny student room without access to your
drinks cupboard/fridge/waitress service, your son is going to
have a twinge of homesickness. Don't assume it just happens to
girls. It doesn't mean your son is becoming a wimp. It's just a natural reaction to being thrust out in the cold, away from a home
he's despised for so long.

Here's what you can do:
- Reassure him that it can take time to find the right friends.
- Remind him of what it was like when he went to his senior
  school and felt alone.
- Encourage him to join societies and clubs. Sports clubs are

great places for meeting people – get him to check out the gym/football pavilion.

After that, it's really up to him. He's a big boy and you can't ask friends round to tea any more so he has someone to play with. The best thing you can do is let him work out the homesickness on his own, while at the same time making it clear that you're there when he needs you. But don't overdo this. You might be missing him so badly that you feel like picking up the phone and ringing him every day. But if you do that, it won't give him a chance to settle. When you chat, don't say how much you're missing him or tell him that the dog is pining. Talk positively about what you've been doing and ask him what he's been up to. Tell him about silly little things that have been happening at home. They might not seem important to you but domestic trivia is much more gripping when you're far away. It will also remind him how boring it is at home and make him glad he's in a more exciting place.

Good old fashioned letters are also nice. My student son made me feel really guilty at the end of his first year by complaining that I was the only parent who hadn't sent packages of food. It didn't matter that he could buy food from the supermarket down the road or even get a decent meal at the union. The point was that he wanted the surprise of a parcel in the post. Which just goes to show that students are really kids at heart.

It's also normal for toddler type separation anxiety to set in. Remember how they used to yell when they were little, if you went out of the room for a minute? They yelled because their basic instincts told them there might be danger if they were out of your sight. Your great big man of a student can suffer the same thing. It's a common psychological pattern that students can panic that their parents are going to be killed in a car crash or have some ghastly accident when they're not there. It's all part of learning to cope on their own. So if they say they're worried, reassure them. Set up an emergency structure so someone in the family can let them know if a disaster does happen. Then they know they won't be kept in the dark. After that, they'll stop worrying so much. (Unless they're training to be a parent.)

TIP

...from the student support department at St Andrews uni: "Tell your student son/daughter that everyone else will be feeling homesick too – it's just that they might not show it."

You could suggest they tell another student how they feel, providing they tell the right person and not someone who'll put them down as a mummy's boy/girl. Hopefully, that other student will say 'That's how I feel too' and wham, bam, they've got a homesick buddy.

WARNING: There are bound to be one or two real Big Issues that happen when he's away. It might be the death of a grandparent or it could be you moving house. Always keep him in the picture and tell him what's going on. Don't be tempted to 'save him' from pain by telling him afterwards. I remember my Godmother died tragically when I was at university and my mother, not wanting to upset me, didn't tell me until after her funeral. I felt cheated because I hadn't been given the opportunity of being there. It also made me wonder what else my mother was hiding from me. So come clean. For more help on this, see Chapter Twenty.

CHAPTER SEVENTEEN

Work, work, work

COURSE DIFFICULTIES

This is every parent's – and student's – worst nightmare (well, one of them). Your daughter will have chosen the university for the course (the ratio of boys to girls had nothing to do with it). So if the course is wrong, they're in the soup. Or are they?

Advise them to hang on for a few weeks. It can take time to bed down when you start anything new. They need to get into the subject properly before making up their mind. If they still feel they've taken the wrong course, they need to see their personal tutor or head of department. Perhaps there's another option on the course they could take instead. Or maybe it's not too late to change subjects altogether. Some universities are more flexible than others on this.

> **TIP**
>
> ...from St Andrews Counselling Service: "Find out if there's a dead-line for changing courses/modules. If there is, try to make up your mind before it expires. It's usually around two to three weeks."

WHERE TO GO FOR GENERAL HELP

You could also get her to check out the pastoral/counselling services. These will be advertised all over hall noticeboards. Some are run by university staff (there's nearly always a professional counsellor on site). Some are run by students (such as Nightline).

But resist the temptation to jump in and talk to someone yourself without getting her permission. She won't thank you for that. If, however, she doesn't mind you talking to someone, you could ring her tutor/department head and suggest a meeting with your daughter present too.

Depending on your religion, you could also encourage her to go to the relevant uni chaplain/rabbi or whoever. You don't have to be a religious freak to do this, and it can be reassuring.

If your daughter is 19 or under, she could get in touch with Connexions, a new government counselling service to help young people discuss any kind of problem including drugs, exam stress, relationships and even difficult, demanding parents...Log onto **www.connexions.gov.uk**.

TIP

Many course difficulties arise from the student not being organised. Get them to write down deadlines and essay briefs. If necessary, provide them with diaries/wall charts/kicks up the butt via emails.

CHANGING UNIVERSITIES

If she really feels the course is all wrong and it's too late to change, she might consider a year out and then starting again. She might actually loathe the university itself and want to go somewhere else. Again, try to make sure she really wants to do this before making such a big move.

Talk to your daughter's old school and ask for guidance on which university and course would be a better alternative. Most schools are keen to help ex-pupils, especially if they're in need. It will probably be too late for this year so your daughter will have to take a year out and reapply through UCAS. It might be that she has to retake A level modules to get different grades for a new course. Again, discuss this with the school.

WILL THEY HAVE TO PAY IF THEY LEAVE?

Aimhigher, the government body to publicise university educa-tion and careers, says: "If your son/daughter is changing courses from one institution to another, you can apply for a refund if you've paid the tuition fees yourself. But if too much time has elapsed, you'll have to wait for the next year to start at a new uni. You also have to reapply through your Local Education Authority for further fee grants at your new chosen uni."

PERSONAL STORIES

Richard, 21, went to Leeds University for one term before deciding he wished he'd gone to Loughborough. "My par-ents weren't very pleased and told me to stick it. But I was really unhappy. I hated the place and I didn't like the course. I came home and worked for a local company for eight months to earn money and save for next year. I reap-plied through UCAS and got a place at Loughborough. Now I'm in my second year and really happy. It's hard to choose the right university at the time and easy to make mistakes."

Gillian, the mother of a second year student who has just left after four terms, advises parents not to push their children towards university if they're not sure in the first place. "Our son was doing Sports Science and decided he didn't see a future for himself in that industry any more. He'd outgrown sport himself and he didn't think it would pay much. Now he's a 'learn as you earn' trainee quantity surveyor with a top international firm. Ironically, it's what he considered doing in the first place, while in the upper sixth."

Fred, a father of a 19 year old daughter who dropped out after six weeks, makes the following point. "Some children really don't like leaving home. I wish she'd given it a bit longer but she missed her home comforts and her boyfriend. Now she's working and very happy. Sometimes I think we must have done something wrong to make her like home so much."

So *can* you overprotect them? "Yes," says family psychologist Dr Pat Spungin, founder of the parenting website **www.raisingkids.co.uk**. "It is possible for parents to over cosset their children so they don't want to leave home. Instead, they need to sell them the idea of going to uni so they're excited by all the social and educational opportunities. Don't start getting all weepy and saying 'I'm really going to miss you.'"

On the other hand, adds Dr Spungin, it's different strokes for different folks. "Some children really are happier at home. In mainland Europe, it's much more common for students to go to uni in their own town and live at home. It's also becoming more common in Britain, particularly in London where it's very expensive to live so many students commute from the suburbs. The problem is that they can miss out on learning to be independent. But this isn't important for everyone."

THE BOYFRIEND BACK HOME v WORK ISSUE

If your daughter is worried about going to uni or is considering dropping out because of the boyfriend at home, try not to panic, says Denise Knowles, counsellor for Relate. "Ask her what the benefits of coming home would be. Ask her what she'd miss about being at university. Remind her of her hopes when she went to uni. And point out that even if she stayed at home, the boyfriend might change – and so might she."

PERSONAL STORIES

Carole, now 43, chose her university at the age of 18 because it was near her boyfriend. The relationship lasted throughout university but she broke it off afterwards. Now, with hindsight, she feels she missed out on normal student life because the commitment of a boyfriend stopped her joining in. "I was terrified my daughter would do the same – and she has. She's just turned down a place at a prestigious university to go to another uni which isn't considered so academic but which is nearer her boyfriend. I'm very upset."

But maybe Carole's daughter isn't so short sighted after all. "Children who are bonders, and need a special friend, can be much happier if they are with people they know," says Dr Spungin. "The important thing is that it doesn't interfere with her education."

Even if it does, it's not the end of the world. Toni, now 20, turned down a place at Durham to stay at home and get engaged to her long term boyfriend. She is now training to be an accountant and seems very happy. "We were disappointed at first," admits her father. "But she's got her career mapped out in front of her. Maybe she'll do a degree later in life."

Try, however, to get your daughter/son to think twice before going to the same uni as their beloved one. "My daughter turned down Oxford for Nottingham because her boyfriend was there already," said one mother. " By the end of the first year, she'd decided she didn't want to be one half of a couple and they broke up."

IS HE WORKING HARD ENOUGH?

Good question. Ideally, you should have got him into a reasonable work pattern when he was at school and living at home. But if the horse has already bolted, this could be too late and you'll have to rely on his own conscience to pull him up at uni. Hopefully, a few duff essay grades, together with the desire to impress the girls at seminars, might also stir him into action.

You can, however, pass your lesson onto younger children still at home, who haven't got to uni stage. "The trick is to stick to a pattern," advises educational psychologist Peter Kendall. "When they get back from school, allow them to unwind and have something to eat before homework. Create a warm, cosy and quiet environment for them to do this. Some children need short breaks between subjects."

Great advice for younger children. But you can hardly do this for an adult child who's not at home for you to check on. You can, however, gently ask him about his working patterns. He needs to work hard but also play hard too. When you talk on the phone, encourage him to strike a balance. If he was bad at handing in work on time at school, point out that this is his chance to start a clean slate. Take an interest in his course and offer to order books for him on Amazon. Find out when his exams are and encourage him to write down dates of exams and essay deadlines in the diary/wallchart you've bought him.

At the end of the day, however, you have to let go. If he doesn't do well, his tutor will tell him in no uncertain terms. Eventually, he'll have to tell you. There comes a time when you can't do everything for your children and this is one of them.

As parents, we also have to accept that they might have different work patterns from ours. We might find it impossible to write a report after partying all night, or to play heavy metal while doing a thesis on the Reformation. But some students really do work better that way. Or they think they do until they get their marks and start rethinking their strategy.

It's also a learning curve for them. For many students, it's their first real taste of freedom and socialising big time. It will take a few false starts at first before they learn how to balance work and play. Then, hopefully, they'll get it right – or near to.

If it all goes wrong and they fail their first year exams, it's time to get tough. If he won't allow you to talk to the tutor, you could ring the university switchboard and ask to be put through to the counselling/pastoral services for advice. It might be that he has to repeat a year. That's not the end of the world. It could be the beginning of a new start.

CHAPTER EIGHTEEN

Sex and drugs and mental health

SEX

You'll have talked about this before but now's a good time to go over a few points. Gently discuss the importance of caring for someone before entering into a serious relationship and of taking precautions. Point out that a lot of their friends might have different ideas on casual relationships. But someone else's views don't have to be yours. I always tell mine that they should look, not just for the X factor, but the whole firework thing when you feel it's bonfire night. That should tell you if it's the right person for you.

Forget their embarrassment – and yours – and talk condoms, morning after pill and everything else.

DRUGS

So your kids wouldn't do them? Check out these statistics. Four per cent of 16-25 year olds have taken ecstacy in the last three months. And 31 per cent of drug related deaths are first time users. "Going to college or uni is one of the danger times when teenagers start doing drugs because they want to be part of the crowd," warns ADFAM, the charity to help users and their families.

"Try picking a quiet time to discuss their views on drugs. Listen with respect and show them your main concern is for their health. Don't fall out, keep communication lines open and tell them you're there for them. Remind them that a drug can have different effects, even if they've taken it before. Point out that cannabis can dull their memory. That it's dangerous to mix drugs with other drugs or alcohol. And that if needles/syringes are shared, infections can spread such as HIV and hepatitis."

Having said all this, many students experiment with cannabis (you may well have done so yourself as a student). So if you get too heavy handed, they might not tell you when they get into deeper waters.

Signs to look out for, especially when you see your child for visits or holidays, include:

- Red eyes/sore throat/runny nose/weight loss – but hasn't had a cold or illness.

- Drops old friends and makes new ones or doesn't bother with friends at all.

- Change in eating/sleeping habits: pot smokers often get the 'munchies' and need to eat voraciously afterwards.

- Different or moody behaviour.

- Loss of interest in school work or outside interests.

- Objects in their room, like spoons discoloured from heating, tin foil, pill boxes, tiny bits of clear food wrap, sugar lumps, syringes or needles, cigarette papers, lighters, cigarette ends made of card, butane gas canisters, shredded cigarettes, pipes, small stickers or transfers, small bottles.

GUIDE TO DIFFERENT DRUGS SO YOU KNOW WHAT THEY'RE TALKING ABOUT

(Information from Frank, the Drugs Helpline for the Department of Health 0800 776600)

COCAINE Other names include coke, charlie, snow, C. It's a white powder snorted up the nose. Sometimes dissolved and injected.

Effect: Gives a sense of well being, alertness and confidence for short time. Users crave more.

Risks: Addictive/users feel tired and depressed afterwards/chest pains and possible fatal heart problems/convulsion.

Law: Class A drug. (Up to seven years imprisonment for possession and unlimited fine. Up to life imprisonment for supplying and unlimited fine.)

CRACK Smokeable form of cocaine. Can also be dissolved and injected. Other names include rock, wash, stone.

Effect: As above but more intense.

Risks: As above.

Law: As above.

CANNABIS Also known as marijuana, draw, blow, weed, puff, shit, hash, ganja, spliff, wacky backy. Comes in different forms: solid dark lump called 'resin'/crushed flower heads and small leaves called 'grass'/stick/dark oil. Can be rolled in spliff or joint, smoked on its own in a special pipe or cooked and eaten in food. Most commonly used drug among 11-25 year olds.

Effect: Users feel relaxed and talkative/can create craving for food (called the 'munchies'). Effect more intense when cooked and eaten.

What every parent should know *before* their child goes to university

Risks: Affects ability to learn and concentrate/tiredness/apathy/lack of motivation/anxiety/paranoia/respiratory diseases like lung cancer.

Law: Recently, the government reclassified it to a Class C drug (maximum imprisonment two years) but possession is still illegal.

SPEED Correct name is amphetamine. Other names include whizz, uppers, amph, bill, sulphate. Comes as grey or white powder that's snorted/swallowed/smoked/injected/ dissolved/tablets.

Effects: Speeds up the mind, making user feel confident and energetic.

Risk: Tension/anxiety/tiredness/depression/panic/hallucinations/heart strain/mental illness.

Law: Class B (class A if prepared for injection).

LSD Also known as acid, trips, tabs, blotters, microdots, dots. Tabs of LSD are small squares of paper, often with a picture on one side. Tabs are swallowed. Can also be taken as tiny tablets (microdots).

Effect: Known as a trip and can last up to 12 hours/surroundings seem very different/sense of movement and time can speed up or slow down/objects, colours and sounds can be distorted.

Risks: Trips can't be stopped/bad trips can be terrifying/flashbacks can happen after the event/mental health problems can be made worse.

Law: Class A.

HEROIN Also known as smack, brown, horse, gear, junk, H, jack, scag. Comes as brownish-white powder which is smoked, snorted or dissolved and injected.

Effects: Gives user a sense of warmth and well being/relaxation and drowsiness.

Risks: Addiction/overdose,coma or death/vein damage/sharing inject- ing equipment can lead to dangerous infections like hepatitits B or C and HIV/AIDS.

Law: Class A.

ECSTASY Also known as E, doves, XTC, disco biscuits, echoes, hug drug, burgers, fantasy. Chemical name is MDMA. Comes as tablets of different shapes, size and colour but often white.

Effects: Users feel alert and happy in their surroundings/sound, colour and emotions seem more intense/can dance for hours.

Risks: tiredness/depression/risk of overheating and dehydration (users should sip a pint of non-alcoholic fluid every hour)/liver and kidney problems/possible brain damage leading to depression.

Law: Class A.

WARNING: Kids and adults often take a second ecstasy tablet because they can't feel the effects of the first one. Then both kick in and the result can be fatal. Bad batches of ecstasy can also contain other substances which can kill.

PMA and 4MTA are two new manmade drugs that are often passed off as E. Frank points out that their effects can be very different and they may take longer to kick in with a risk of double-dosing to compensate (and double the side effects).

GASES, GLUES AND AEROSOLS Misuse of products like gas lighter refills, aerosols, glue, paints etc. Users sniff them or spray into back of throat.

Effects: Like being drunk/thick-headed/dizzy/dreamy/hallucinations.

Risks: Nausea/vomiting/blackouts/fatal heart problems/damage to brain, liver and kidneys.

Law: Illegal for retailers to sell to under 18s if they suspect it could be used wrongly.

TRANQUILLISERS Product names include Valium, Ativan, Mogadon (moggies), Librium etc. Tablets, capsules, injections or suppositories.

Effects: Calms users and slows them down mentally/relieves anxiety and tension/causes drowsiness and forgetfulness.

Risks: Addictive/dangerous if mixed with alcohol/loss of short term memory/panic attacks when users try to quit/dangerous if contents are injected.

Law: The supply of these is against the law. Class C penalties.

NAME GAME

Drugs have so many different names that it's hard to know what's what. But if you hear your teenager talking about some of these, it's time for action:

- Rainbows =LSD
- Ram = poppers
- Red Mitsubishi = PMA
- Resin = cannabis
- Rhubarb and custard = ecstasy
- Rock = crack
- Roofies/rugby balls = tranquilisers
- H/hawk = heroin

THEY COULD GO TO PRISON – AND SO COULD YOU

A first time offender might receive a formal warning/formal caution. If a child between 10 and 17 commits further offences, they could be charged and dealt with by a Youth Court which could then fine parents/put the child in a Young Offenders Institution. If you know your child is taking drugs at home, you may also be charged. Maximum penalties for drug users can be up to seven years imprisonment and/or a fine.

ALCOHOLISM

Drink can be a huge problem amongst students, and there are some scary sporting traditions such as so-called dirty pints which consist of several shots of different spirits. Your son/daughter might say you're fussing but there's a thin line between heavy drinking and alcoholism.

The best way to make your point is to give them the statistics. Four or more units can endanger your health. A shot of spirit/glass of wine is one unit and half a pint is one unit too. The body takes one hour to clear one unit. Makes you think, not drink. Maybe we should use that as a slogan.

Point out that binge drinking – officially defined as five or more drinks in one session – can lead to brain damage. A new survey by the University of Memphis shows that adolescent rats exposed to high doses of alcohol had impaired growth and altered brain function. The US researchers say the same could happen to teenagers because their bodies are going through a unique developmental period where binge drinking can have long lasting implications

Also go over points which you will probably have already made during their teenage years. (There's no harm in a quick refresher course.) Alcohol clouds your mind so you might end up sleeping with someone you don't really like or telling your best friend you hate her. Stick to a limited number and never put your drink down in case someone spikes it. Don't assume alcopops are weak. You know it. They should know it by now. But you can still tell them again. At the time of going to press, Tony Blair was having a binge drinking campaign – against it, that is, not for it. Makes you wonder if having a student son has shown him just how much younger people drink nowadays for a good night out. (Some of us oldies do it too but that's *our* business....)

Drinking too much is becoming a serious student problem. All you can do is suggest they stick to a certain number of drinks and know when to stop. There comes a time when we have to step back and let them make their own mistakes. The important bit is being there for them if and when they shout.

TIP

Don't panic too much about drink, says the student support service at St Andrews: "Parents often think that uni is all about drink and sex. It's not like that all the time. In fact, we're pleasantly surprised."

TAKING UP SMOKING

This is another addiction which often happens when kids go to uni, partly so they become one of the crowd and partly because they think it relieves stress. Point out that smoking doesn't just give you cancer – it can give you a heart attack too. Get an older sibling/friend of the family to tell them that smoking is a turn off when it comes to kissing. (They're more likely to believe someone other than their parents who have forgotten what lips were made for.)

Don't go nuts if you find they're smoking – they're adults after all – but show them how they can stop. Take them down to the supermarket where there's an array of over the counter nicotine patches. And contact **www.quit.org.uk**. You could give them a copy of White Ladder's book *The Voice of Tobacco* which should give them a laugh as well as helping them to quit (available at **www.whiteladderpress.com**).

CONTACTS

For useful resources if you want to know more about drugs or alcohol, please see the listing on our website **www.whiteladderpress.co.uk**, alongside the information about this book.

SUICIDE AND DEPRESSION

One in 10 teenagers self-harm, according to the Samaritans. And men are more likely to commit suicide than women in the 15-24 year age group. Like alcoholism and drugs, the danger of suicide and depression increases when 'kids' go to uni and feel they can't cope. Susan Quilliam, agony aunt, gives the following advice on behalf of the Samaritans: "Look out for physical symptoms, like sleeping/eating more or less than usual. Also for mental symptoms like loss of concentration and interest. Be aware of emotional symptoms such as tears or panic attacks and excessive drinking or smoking. Look out for self-deprecating comments like 'I know I'll never pass'. Be sensitive to calls for help such as hanging around, and wanting to talk."

If you spot any of these, give them practical support like taking food up and maybe having them home for the weekend to cosset them. Listen without feeling you have to find on the spot cures or give advice. Don't add to their stress by blaming them or yourself or panicking. And contact the Samaritans or encourage them to contact Nightline, the student counselling service.

Also try to listen to their financial worries. New research by Bath and Exeter universities suggest that students who are worried about getting into debt are also more likely to suffer from depression. So instead of bawling them out when they get overdrawn, help them find an action plan.

CULTS

If they come home at the weekend looking like a Hari Krishna follower, you might need a chat. It's very easy for kids to be swayed by groups at uni that offer a protection against the scariness of being alone. The problem is that they're an adult now, and you can't tell them what to believe in. You can, however, point out why their behaviour might cause problems for them. For example, a cult that stops them seeing their family will hurt everyone. But if your child is heavily into this, they probably won't listen to reason. So it's time to find professional help. Again, check out our list of contact numbers and resources at **www.whiteladderpress.com** alongside the information about this book.

CHAPTER NINETEEN

Physical health

DIET

Are they eating the right food? Probably not, but you can still give them some guidelines. I wish someone had done that for me so I wouldn't have been a plump student. (I lost my weight in my early twenties but that's another story.) Try to get them to eat healthily with salads, brown bread, protein and so on. If they're self-catering, suggest they cook with other people on the corridor sometimes. Ask them casually what they've had to eat that night when you ring them up. If they are existing on baguettes or noodle packets, suggest they vary their diet. Remind them that it's important to drink – we're talking water and juice here.

"Suggest they buy a wholemeal sandwich instead of junk food," advises Zoe Harcombe, author of *Why Do You Overeat When All You Want Is To Be Slim?* (£9.99, Accent Press). "Encourage them to make a quick pasta sauce – there's a recipe in the book – and to make their own salad with an iceberg lettuce and pack of tomatoes instead of buying pre-packed salad. Also suggest they try porridge for breakfast. It's a great food for students because it's brain food – it releases carbohydrates slowly and they won't want to snack."

TIP

Teach them basic cleanliness techniques such as to wash drying up cloths regularly/wipe work surfaces down with a clean cloth. Send them up with cleaning materials in case there aren't enough in communal kitchens/bathrooms etc.

BULIMIA/ANOREXIA

Zoe Harcombe went through this herself so she knows what she's talking about. "When students go to uni, they finally have the choice to eat what they want, when. So it's almost impossible for parents to have any control. Ideally, a few years earlier, parents need to stop forcing the food issue and allow children to eat what they want when they want, within reason."

DIET AND EXERCISE

Uni is sometimes known as the 10 pound part of your life because many students put on 10 pounds during their time there. "Encourage your student to exercise," advises Zoe. "And warn them against snacking on junk during the evening when they're writing late night essays. If they're hungry, how about a piece of chocolate that's a minimum 70 per cent cocoa?"

TIP

Encourage them to check out the uni gym. Great way for meeting people too.

SERIOUS ILLNESS

Tragically, this does happen. And it's not always easy to pick up the tell tale signs if they're away for long. That's why it's good to see them at least twice a term. Look out for signs like paleness, puffy eyes, tiredness, change in weight and so on. You can't *make* them go to the medical centre but you can do your best.

It's not a bad idea to get them checked over by the family doctor during the summer holiday. Even if your son is now a temporary resident, he is still entitled to this. An increasing number of adults are now having regular health checks through BUPA or the like. Even if you're not medically insured privately, you can still pay for this.

If your son misses work because of illness, make sure he's told his tutor. It's not out of order for you to ring yourself and explain the situation. Better that than them not realising there was a genuine excuse for an essay not being handed in on time.

JUST NOT FEELING WELL

It's a horrible feeling when your daughter rings and says she feels a bit hot and she's got a headache and by the way, she feels sick as well. Try to get her to go to the medical centre – explain, without alarming her, that it could be serious so it's important to get it checked out.

On the other hand, you don't want to make a fuss. "Jamie got really bad flu during his second term," says his dad George. "We were pretty sure it was flu and nothing worse so we told him to take paracetamol and drink a lot. He still wasn't better the following week so we went up to see him. We stayed a day – and then got flu ourselves!"

Try to make sure your student has a rough idea of what to do if they are sick/throw a temperature/have a headache. Tell them what the symptoms of meningitis are (headache, nauseousness, aversion to light and usually, later, a rash). Give them a first aid kit and tell them to contact someone if they feel really bad. Run over basic first aid techniques such as running cold water on a burn. Even better, send them on a first aid course.

TIP

Make sure your student has had a meningitis jab before going to uni. Some schools do this routinely between the ages of 13 and 17, but not all. Meningitis can spread between young people. So too can glandular fever, sometimes known rather unfairly as the 'kissing disease' even though you don't need to snog anyone to get it. Symptoms include raised glands, temperature and lethargy.

CHAPTER TWENTY

Changes at home

The funny thing about a teenager is that they spend years telling you how much they hate home and can't wait to get away from it. Then they get all upset if you make the smallest of changes such as getting a new carpet or moving to the other end of the country. Still, who said teenagers (or parents) were ever easy?

The golden rule is to tell them about any changes which are happening at home. Keep them abreast of news during those phone calls or emails. It goes without saying that big changes are best said, rather than emailed, because a proper voice is essential to cope with the reaction.

BAD NEWS

The overriding message from all the experts here is simple. Be honest. Otherwise, they won't trust you when they do find out what's happened/is going on. So tell your student as soon as possible if someone has died or is ill or getting divorced. If you don't, they will worry in the future about things going wrong again. If possible, go up and tell them in person. Letters and phone calls can be too distant and upsetting.

"Whoops, meant to tell you, I've cancelled your train ticket home to Devon for the holidays because we've moved to Aberdeen"

DIVORCE

"Parents often think, quite wrongly, that it's OK to get divorced when their children go to university because it won't affect them so much," warns Denise Knowles, counsellor for Relate. "In fact, it's very hard on students because they're away from home and don't know what's going on. They may be old enough to vote but they're not necessarily old enough to cope with the news that mum and dad aren't going to be together any more. They're going into an unknown situation (uni) and are coming back to an unknown situation (a broken home)."

Remember too, adds Denise, that it's not just the disintegration of your marriage that will upset them. It's also the discovery that home isn't the same any more. "If you have to move house because of the breakdown, it can be very disturbing for a student who is looking forward to coming back to a familiar environment after the unfamiliarity of a new uni. Even if you don't move house, it won't be the same because one of the parents won't be there any more."

Sometimes, it's actually best to make the break earlier – or later. "There is never a good time for divorce," says Denise. "But waiting until the children go to university isn't necessarily ideal."

But whenever you do it, it's the *way* you do it that matters. "If you go down to uni to break the news, make sure your child has friends and support around them," advises Denise. "Try to leave your emotional angst behind and concentrate on the practicalities. Children – and that includes students – need to know details like where they'll be living. Resist the temptation to give them details of your partner's affair unless they ask questions. And even then, don't enter into a tit for tat argument in front of your student child."

> ### TIP
>
> Get a kindly family friend to visit them and keep in touch during your divorce. They could be a sounding board for your son or daughter who might not be able to tell you how they're feeling.

Be aware too that an older child at uni might pump a younger one at home for information. "Tell your older child that you are happy to give them any information they want. Reassure them of your love. But be prepared for your student to be angry with you even if you are the 'innocent' party. The anger comes because their life has been disrupted and sometimes this anger can take time to pass."

PERSONAL STORY

"Don't assume that because your kids are adults, they can cope with all the details of their father's affair or their mother's alliances," says Jan, a third year student whose parents split up at the end of her first year. "Each of my parents told me lurid details about the other and I couldn't take it. Now I prefer not to see either of them – but I feel cheated of a home especially when I see friends who've got normal families at home."

THEY DIDN'T GIVE ME THE PRACTICAL STUFF

Before telling them you're splitting, get the practical details sorted out such as future funding for uni and where they can live (if they choose) in the holidays. "When my parents divorced at the end of my second year at uni, they told me I'd have to fund my own way through uni," says Sam, a third year student at

Loughborough. "In fact, my tutor helped me obtain a full grant – something my parents could have discovered for themselves from a simple phone call to the local education authority."

Denise Knowles from Relate adds that it's also important that you don't allow them to shoulder the responsibility for younger siblings – or for your own problems. "My father used to come down to my uni on the pretext of visiting me but then use my room as a bolt hole because he said it was the only place he could go to for peace," said Max, now 25. "It might sound pathetic but even at 20, I was the one who needed reassurance. But I was having to act like my dad's father."

Maria, 22, a recent graduate from York, used to get really upset when she rang home and frequently found her mother in tears over her impending divorce. "It was the worst thing I had ever had to cope with. I wanted to be there to help her but I was too far away."

It's natural for a parent to get upset when your marriage is breaking up. But just as you shouldn't cry in front of young children, don't cry in front of your absent student, down the phone. Ring back when you're calmer.

TIP

Write to your student's tutor and tell them what is happening at home.

DEATH OF A PARENT

This is a terrible thing to happen to any child but, like divorce, when it happens if a student is away, they feel even more out of control and panicky.

What every parent should know *before* their child goes to university

If you or your partner is seriously ill, you should tell your student son or daughter, says Annie Kiffwood, spokesperson for Cruse, the charity that helps the bereaved. "A student is not a child so they need to know what is happening. If you just let the bad news trickle out, it will lead to mistrust and they may well resent you. Warn them that the illness is serious and possibly life threatening. If they don't know all the facts, they can't make decisions – and students need to be able to do that. They might decide to take a break from their course in order to come home and be with that ill person. It's important to let them do that if they want."

Annie speaks from personal experience as her own mother died of cancer during her time at university. "I came home to nurse her and took my degree a year late. But it was the right thing to do for me and it would have been wrong if anyone had tried to stop me. Someone who is 18 plus should be allowed to make their own decisions. Parents can be too overprotective even if they mean well."

Similarly, it's vital to tell your student about the death of anyone close to them at home. "Get them home as soon as possible," advises Annie. "When they're away, their imagination can make it far worse for them. At home, they will be surrounded by people who care and who knew the person. The Army, Navy and RAF usually bring a bereaved member of staff home as soon as possible, partly for humanitarian reasons but also because they can't do their jobs properly if they are grieving away from their families. It's the same for students. They can't work properly unless they are given a chance to grieve in the right place."

HOW TO HELP THEM

Try to get your student to talk to their tutor. "It's important that the tutor knows what's going on in case it affects the student's marks,'" says Annie. "In my particular case, I had a wonderful tutor who had been through the same thing although I didn't know it then."

If your student refuses to do this, don't force them. Yes, it's being pushy and they won't thank you for it. You could gently nudge them in the direction of Nightline, a student counselling service that exists in most unis. Or give them the website of Cruse's service for young people who have been bereaved. **www.rd4u.co.uk** . The website is staffed by younger members of Cruse who give advice online. Alternatively, ring the free helpline for young people on 0808 8081677.

If your student 'child' retreats into a shell, you have to be patient, adds Annie. "Too many people try to help the bereaved by doing what *they* would want people to do for them. But everyone is different. Your adult child needs time on his own to come to terms with his grief and all the other emotions which are so individual."

You could try to get family friends or older siblings to help but at the end of the day, you can only do so much. Sadly, losing someone is part of growing up. On the other hand, if you feel they are going to hurt themselves, go to your GP immediately.

WHEN A FRIEND AT UNI DIES

"This is a terrible experience for students because they are part of such a close knit community," points out Annie. "But don't insist they come home so you can comfort them. They are better off staying with their uni friends who will understand more than you, because they knew the person. When families in the UK had sons or daughters who survived 9/11, they wanted them to come home so they could hug them and physically feel they were there.

But the grown up children wanted to stay in the States because they needed to take part in the grieving process. It's very dangerous to interrupt that."

TELL THEM ABOUT THE GOOD THINGS TOO

Of course they're going to miss out on big happy events like grandad's eightieth. But give them the chance of coming even if you know they're too far away or busy. Otherwise, they'll feel cut off and excluded. If they don't get to the birthday party or wedding or whatever, send them photographs. Get them to teach you how to do it digitally on the computer if you can't do it yourself.

Encourage them to stay part of the family by reminding them of family birthdays and big occasions. That way they can send a card or make a phone call. It's nice for grandad, too, to know that his grandson remembers...

CHANGING ROOMS

Resist the temptation to give his room a makeover without consulting him first. Even if you do, it might be best to wait until he's home. He might say he fancies a change of wallpaper but then hate the one you've put up while he's been away. For some strange reason, security is still important to your student daughter and son. So much is changing in their lives, that home becomes more of an important feature than it might have been before. It's the one thing that needs to stay still – for a while at least, until they cope with adulthood.

Similarly, be careful about moving other children into your student's room. It might seem the logical move, especially if your youngest three are sharing a room and the eldest is bursting to inhabit the new spare room. But the truth is that it isn't spare, is it? It belongs to someone else – and the holidays will soon be here.

MOVING HOUSE

This might seem like a good time but talk it over with your absent student. Find out their feelings and involve them in just the same way that you would if they were at home. If possible, get your student to look at the new house before you make decisions. You might not allow them to influence the final move but it's all part of that psychological process of making them feel as though they are still in the family. Which, of course, they are.

CHAPTER TWENTY ONE

So you're home alone

Your student child has been part of your marriage or relationship for so long, that it's bound to alter things when that child has gone. It's a tricky time and one where there are no easy answers. The best advice is not to rush into decisions. You might feel that now the glue of children has gone, there's little to hold you together. But if you stick fast for a while, you might discover that other things hold you together instead. It's a bit like telling your child to hang on in university. He might like it more, as time goes by.

"Share your feelings and don't keep them to yourselves," says Denise Knowles of Relate. "Don't immediately give up if you feel you have nothing in common any more. Make an effort to go out or do something new together. Take up squash or play tennis again. It's not easy but it can be done. You might be pleasantly surprised. Or you might have to face up to some tough truths."

STILL MARRIED BUT YOU'RE DIFFERENT – THE EFFECT ON YOU

Your child has gone but that doesn't mean she doesn't need you any more. So if you've been the primary carer, don't declassify yourself as redundant. Use this time to do all those things you yearned to do when she was at home and you couldn't. Exercise, when you find yourself getting depressed. This releases endorphins, the so-called happy hormones. Plan things to do for you and any remaining children at home.

PERSONAL STORY

Jasmine found it helped to list two or three activities a week for her and her remaining daughter to do. "It gave a structure to our lives and gradually it seemed less odd to do something without my son."

COMPLETELY ALONE

If you don't have a partner and your last child has flown the nest, this could be your opportunity to fly yourself. Think of things you've always wanted to do but have been stopped by parental responsibility. How about changing jobs/retraining/working abroad/doing a degree. The possibilities are endless – and many other parents would love to be in your position.

Anthea, 40, retrained as an air hostess when her only son left for uni. "I'd been working part time as an administrator and saw an advert for a low budget airline that wanted staff for domestic flights. I don't have any overnight stays so I'm around during the holidays for my son. But it's shown me a completely new side of life. I can't believe how happy and fulfilled I feel. And it's a good example for my son too who has seen that you can make big changes even at my age."

PERSONAL STORY

John and Denise booked up a series of plays and concerts to go to after their last child went to uni. "We made the bookings *before* she went, so we had something to look forward to."

CONTACTS

There are organisations which might be able to help you rethink your life now your student has flown. Check out the listings on our website at **www.whiteladderpress.com** alongside the information about this book.

"Hmm. I wonder whether a school swimming certificate and a GCSE in Art would be enough to get me the job?"

CHAPTER TWENTY TWO

Visiting – your place or mine?

HOW SOON?

Give your student at least four weeks on her own before you suggest visiting or a weekend home. She needs time to settle and if she sees you before then, she might suddenly realise she's missing the cat/Sky/your homemade lasagne too much to go back to uni.

Visiting rights obviously depend on how far away the university is. We know a family whose boys were at Oxford, only half an hour from home. Those boys came home at least two weekends a month, partly because their mother expected them to. They missed out on a lot of social life especially as Oxford terms are only eight weeks long.

Similarly, if your son is a long way off, that's going to make visiting and weekends home more difficult. Try to strike a happy balance by organising two or so meetings a term. Fix the dates in advance so you both have something to look forward to – or avoid on their part with a last minute excuse.

IS THAT REALLY YOU?

Be prepared for changes when you see her. You will both have changed, even in that short space of time. It's not just that her hair is now a different colour or that she's fatter/thinner/wearing new clothes that she's blown her grant on. She'll be more independent and grown up. And it might take time for the two of you to establish the rapport you had before. This is normal. It's rather like a husband who's been abroad and has now returned. Awkward at first but, pretty soon, you get back into the swing of things. If you didn't have a great relationship before, use this meeting as a new start. Your daughter has changed. You might get on better now.

Respect these changes as much as you can. You might not approve of her hair or new habits like smoking. But she is an adult and if you treat her as such, she's more likely to stay in touch with you. Having said that, it's a standing joke in our house that as soon as our son comes home in the holidays I book him a haircut.

Visiting your daughter for the first time might be awkward, so don't be too disappointed. She'll be (hopefully) pleased to see you but she'll also feel odd because you're on her territory. She'll be terrified you'll say something embarrassing to her friends and she doesn't want you to fuss over her. So be cool about it. Give her a hug but don't slobber over her, saying how much you've missed her. Stick to neutral ground and get her to show you around the university and town. Doing things together takes the heat off the emotional bit, whether you're still talking or not.

Giving her a treat is a clever move too. It's amazing how a slap-up meal at a restaurant can break the ice after a gap. If you go back to her room for coffee, resist the temptation to wash those mugs which have been sitting under the bed for weeks and now resemble the Dead Sea inside.

Resist also the temptation to tell her the room is a mess. If you have to tidy up, do so discreetly. It will only be a mess again when you've left and all you'll have achieved is denting her confidence. You could, however, make subtle suggestions. Would she like you to take anything home for washing? Is there anything she needs?

Make friends with her mates. If you're nice to them and maybe take them out for a meal too, they'll speak warmly of you later. And then your daughter might realise you're not so bad after all. Try not to be shocked or disapproving of them. Your daughter is an adult. She needs to work out for herself who is a friend and who isn't. On the other hand, it's good to show you are always there for her if things go wrong – and that includes friends who might not be as nice as she'd thought.

If she wants to talk about boyfriends, listen without making too many judgments unless she asks for them. Whatever you say will eventually be held against you. Don't keep pressing her for details of her social life. Did you tell your parents everything at that age? Exactly. Parents nowadays are so hands-on and keen to improve their child's progress that they often want to know too much.

Don't overstay your welcome. A day's visit is usually enough unless it's a long way. When we go to Scotland, which is where one of our children is at uni, we usually stay in a B&B outside the town to give him space. Our other two children, on the other hand, have stayed in his student house and had a fantastic time.

VISITS HOME

The first visit home is going to be full of expectation – on both sides. Mandy, 18, says she couldn't wait to see her younger sister even though they had never got on particularly well. "When she opened the door, I gave her a big hug and asked if she'd missed me. She stared at me and said 'You've only been gone for six weeks.' After that, I just wanted to go back to uni. I felt hurt because I didn't think they'd missed me."

Because you both have possibly unreal expectations, it's difficult to get it right. My son always jokes that he knows he's really home when we've had our first good row and can be normal again. There's some truth in this. See it from their point of view. Your daughter is excited about being back but life is different. Her uni friends aren't there and she's missing them already, after a few hours. You are excited about having her back but she's not the same girl that went away. She's learned to live life on her terms. When you want to go to bed, she might just be getting up. There's a queue for the shower. She doesn't fancy the meal you've just spent hours preparing for her because she doesn't eat meat any more (didn't she tell you?). And she's livid with you because you forgot to mention the goldfish died the week after she left.

The trick is to respect their new needs. If she doesn't eat meat, that's her choice. If she goes to bed later than you, she's an adult. On the other hand, she needs to understand that there are other people in the house too so it's not fair to play loud music until 3am.

It's also only fair if she tells you what time she's likely to be in at, when she goes out. The irony is that although you (hopefully) no longer lie awake at night during term time, wondering if she's back, you will worry when she's home and still out at night. That's understandable. You're quite within your rights to ask for an approximate return time.

By the time you've sorted all this out, it will be time for her to go back. But the good news is that next time she's home, it won't seem so strange.

CHAPTER TWENTY THREE

Holiday time

No sooner have you packed her off to uni, than it's time to pack her back home. Packing is the operative word. If you're collecting her yourself, you might expect her to have packed but you'll have a very organised child if that's actually the case. Take extra suitcases with you and boxes to fit in everything she hasn't managed to squeeze in at her end.

TIP

Ring her several days before packing up time and make her get in cardboard boxes from local supermarkets. If she leaves it until the day before, other students will have got them first. I speak from experience.

Don't expect to make a quick getaway. It will take her ages to say goodbye to friends whom she's only known for 10 weeks but whom she seems much closer to than you. Try not to chivvy her along or you'll get off to a bad start. Teenagers aren't usually great at change – and there've been quite a few of these since A levels.

The good thing about holidays is that unlike weekends, which are over before you've ironed out any problems, there's the luxury of time. Don't ruin it with too much nagging. Start to enjoy your new grown up child. Look for the positives and take comfort from her company. Laugh with her and it will encourage her to tell you about her life. Then you can start the nagging bit and tell her that she can jolly well make her own bed...

Make your home open to student visitors, however limited your space. You'll make a better relationship with your child if she feels comfortable about bringing friends home. If she wants to share her bedroom with her boyfriend, be practical. Since she's raised the issue, she's probably doing it at uni anyway. If you don't like her new friends, don't jump in and say so. Offer her gentle guidelines later but let her make up her own mind or you could alienate her.

> **TIP**
>
> Be prepared for weird behaviour. Being home is nice but 'weird nice' as my son puts it. Don't underestimate how much they are missing their friends. They'll need time and understanding to get used to being at home again. Then, just as they do, guess what – it's term time once more.

THIS ISN'T A DOSS HOUSE

Some parents expect their child to pay rent during holiday time. That's up to you but don't be too tough if you want them to come back next time. If they're working, a nominal payment towards food or petrol might be in order. Talking of work, you might need to encourage your student to get a job. It's not just the money – it's also important experience and it looks better on his CV when he finally gets round to applying for a proper job.

If he's not interested, get some forms from the local supermarket and shove them under his nose. Or help him find more interesting alternatives. My son is going to Camp America this summer as a helper in children's camps.

Contact Bunac for overseas holiday jobs (and some London ones) on 0207 251 1152 or **operations@bunac.org.uk**

TIPS

- Take their suitcases/black bags down to the launderette and apologise for the cheesy smell inside. It will save your time and your washing machine's ball bearings.

- Be prepared for the house 'filling up' with all the extras they bring back, eg computer, new clothes (so that's where their grant went). It's rather like having a house guest but worse because they're rude to you and don't bring a gift.

MEETING UP WITH OLD FRIENDS

Your daughter will obviously want to meet up with old school friends. But she might find it strange because they will have changed and so will she. She could need you on hand to offload on. Sympathise and tell her how you've felt when this has happened to you.

EFFECT ON THE FAMILY

Having got used to the change in family dynamics when she left, you now have to get used to an extra person when she's back. Whatever you do, don't tell her it was easier when she wasn't here. And if one of the other children says the same thing, stop them right there. She, of course, is perfectly entitled to tell you that she wishes she'd never come back for the holidays. Just remember that she doesn't really mean it.

LOOK ON THE BRIGHT SIDE

OK, so she's hard work in the holidays but she can help you out. Maybe she could house sit while you're away on the family holiday that she didn't want to go on. Or perhaps she could take one of the younger children out for the day.

WHAT IF HE DOESN'T WANT TO COME HOME FOR THE HOLIDAYS?

Don't take personal offence. He's growing up. He's made new friends and understandably he wants to explore life. He might want to stay up at university or spend the whole holiday at a friend's house. This doesn't mean he doesn't want anything to do with you, although there might be an element of that (see Arguments in Chapter Twenty four below). It means that you've succeeded in creating an independent adult who has the confidence to forge his own way in life.

CHAPTER TWENTY FOUR

More teething problems

ARGUMENTS

Just because you're related to someone, it doesn't mean you are close. It's sad but a fact of life. You might not have got on particularly well with your student child before they left for uni. Now, maybe, the absence has driven you further apart.

The trick – as in any parent/child relationship, whatever age – is to keep the lines of communication open. You might both have said or done things you regret. You might both feel the other has been unfair. You might both be adults. But you are older than he is so it's up to you to be there if he feels like making up.

You can do this in subtle ways. Write the odd postcard. Pay an unexpected visit. Send a small cheque. Bribery worked when they were little and it's not giving in to do it now. It's simply showing that whatever they think (and however you feel at times), you do care.

When I was at university, one of my friends decided to leave during her second year. Three weeks later, her mother called us because she hadn't been able to get hold of her daughter. She hadn't even realised she'd left the course. To this day, I never heard from my friend again and I don't know what happened to her. It still haunts me. But how on earth did her mother feel?

There are organisations like the Salvation Army which can sometimes track people down. But try to stop this before it happens. However difficult your student child is, don't fall out so badly that they just take off and don't come back for years. It simply isn't worth it.

If you really can't reach a compromise, try to get a family friend to talk to him. Explain that you don't want this situation to continue. There are also student counselling organisations like Nightline which could help your student child work through his problems.

PLAYING TOO HARD

If you haven't been able to get hold of your daughter for weeks, or her room mate says she's out for the twentieth night in a row, it might be time to have a quiet word about overdoing it. But be careful. Socialising hard in the first year is natural. It's their first time away from home and suddenly, instead of one party a month, there's something going on every night.

You could, however, gently enquire if she's up to date with essay deadlines. She might tell you to mind your own business but it will hopefully jog her memory. Ask her what kind of grades she's getting. Again, she might not tell you but it might kick that guilt streak into action. One of the hardest things about your child going to university is that there isn't a homework diary for you to look through any more. You can't flick through her files and check what essay mark she got on Lear.

But that's exactly what growing up is all about. She needs to learn for herself – and if she doesn't, her personal tutor will tell her. All you can do is gently point out that university life is a mixture of play *and* work.

WORKING TOO HARD

So you've got a geek. They can be just as hard work as the perpetual partygoer. (Personally speaking, I was a geek during the week and a partygoer at weekends.) If your daughter is still at her laptop at 2am when any self-respecting student is at the union, you might need to pay a visit.

A levels should have taught them how to divide their time meaningfully but maybe there's a problem. Is the work too hard? Is she doing too much work that she doesn't actually need to do? Suggest she talks this over with her personal tutor or friends. Try to get her to go to the university medical centre to check she's not overdoing it.

The stress of being somewhere new can actually bring out the neurosis in some students. Amy's daughter, now in her second year, was always a sensitive child. But when she came home after her first term at uni, Amy noticed that she was developing compulsive tendencies. "She kept checking the front door was locked and seemed to have rituals which she had to follow like putting her left shoe on before her right." Amy persuaded her daughter to go to her family GP and talk things over. Eventually, after several heart to hearts with him and Amy, the daughter confessed that she found it strange being away from home and was often lonely because she hadn't found good friends. The rituals appeared to comfort her.

Amy still didn't feel any better. How was she going to help her daughter make friends when she was so far away? In the end, the daughter sorted it out for herself. At her brother's suggestion, she joined some university clubs and met people with whom she had more in common. As soon as she had something else to fill her mind, she forgot her rituals.

DISCOVERING SEX

Despite what you read, there are several teenagers who go to university never having had sex. (Just as well, really.) So as I said earlier, however embarrassing it is for both of you, it's time for a quick refresher chat. You probably did this at the age of eight when the National Curriculum suggests children ought to start being aware of these things. But now it's far more pertinent. Don't just talk condoms and morning after pill and HIV. Talk emotion too and the importance of really loving someone before you have a full relationship with them.

Whatever your feelings, don't be a prude. You need to keep those communication lines open so you're there to confide in if or when things go wrong. Aileen's daughter Jenny rang at the end of her second year to say she was unexpectedly pregnant. The father was her long term boyfriend but neither wanted to get married. "I was really upset at first but then I realised she needed support, not hysteria. I drove up to her and we talked through the options. She wanted to keep the baby and I must admit I was relieved at that because I'm not sure she could have coped with an abortion. We made an appointment together to see the counselling service and they told us about the back-up help she could get from the university. For example, allowances would be made when she took her finals (by which time her son was three months). There was also a creche and accommodation for parents. It's all so much more civilised than in my day when it would have been disastrous for a student to have got pregnant."

DOESN'T GO TO LECTURES

The freedom of university can be very heady at first, especially if your student child is studying a subject where there are very few lectures. It will take him time to realise that he is still expected to work and to use this free time to do research and background reading. You can help by reminding him of this every now and then.

If he casually mentions that he never goes to lectures, this is the time to say something. Point out that he may be grown up and living away from home, but he still has responsibilities. You are paying for his student lifestyle and you don't expect him to squander it.

There's a huge gulf between having them at home to do A levels and having them far away at university. But that doesn't mean you have to give up responsibility as a parent altogether. So an occasional kick up the proverbial is well within your rights.

Tutorials, by the way, are something else. A student is definitely meant to attend these so if your student scallywag mentions he's missing them too, it's time for a big talk. And a few threats about the grant too, perhaps?

HATES TUTOR

Tough. No one says you have to like your teacher. But try diplomacy. Remind him how he hated his geography teacher. And his history teacher. And the maths teacher too. Could it, by any chance, be him rather than the teacher? Point out that you don't particularly like your boss either but that the trick of being grown up is to get on with those whom you'd really prefer not to be with (this doesn't apply to marriage). Sympathise up to a point but suggest that if he tries really hard with the tutor in question, that tutor might just recognise that he's making an effort and then do the same.

Of course, some tutors are impossible. That's because they'd rather be doing Serious Research than teaching students who are bleary eyed from the night before. But cheer up. One day they'll be famous, and then your son can claim he was taught by him at university before he dropped out.

CHAPTER TWENTY FIVE

Going back to the second year – and the third

Weird isn't it? This time last year, you were both about to kill each other with the strain of going away from home for the first time (unless he went to boarding school and is used to being away from you). Now here you are, a year later, and you're still edgy about the impending departure. Your student might be deeply relieved he's finally able to escape out of your madhouse. Or he might be concerned at going back after getting used to being at home all summer. That's because very few kids of this age like change. He wants to go and he doesn't. Just like last year. So basically, you can't win. Having established that, you might just ignore the tide of hormonal chaos that is swirling around you and remind yourself that in a few weeks time, life will be back to normal again.

HANG ON A MINUTE

Each year brings its own changes. And although your student's tutors will have told her about them, she might not have been listening – or probably wasn't even there, as she would have been recovering from the night before. So ask if she's got a reading list for the next term. Ideally, you should have done this during the holidays in time to order the appropriate books but, if not, there's always good old Amazon. Check what else she's meant to know. You may not feel it's politically correct to go through her things for official looking bits of paper that tell you but on the other hand, it might just save her skin. It's the equivalent of going through her school bag to find out what notes she should have given you weeks ago, and which bear 'Please reply by such and such a date at the latest'.

Depending on the subject your student is doing, each year has its own ups and downs. At the risk of sounding boring, you could use this opportunity for a small pep talk. The second year of a third year course is usually the best. That's because your child has normally settled down, knows where the local clubs are and still assumes that university life goes on for ever.

Now's the time to point out that it's not wise to slack. She might not have finals this year but it will make a big difference – either way – if she stops working or doesn't do enough. So enjoy that second year but remember to keep slogging away in between pints.

THIRD YEAR

Crunch time – unless they're language students (see Year Out section below). How you tackle this depends on your child. If you've got a sensitive flower, you'll need to reassure him that providing he works, he'll be fine during finals. Remember how you had to reassure him when he went into panic mode during GCSEs and A levels? Well it's the same now except you have to do it long distance. The golden rules are to keep in touch and visit every now and then to make sure everything's OK.

Look out for signs of serious stress (see Chapter 26). If you're worried, try to get your offspring to visit their medical centre. Many students are on tranquillisers and it shouldn't be seen as shameful.

"You mean I'm supposed to go back again? I've already done a whole year…"

At the same time, it's not a bad idea to talk jobs. Does he have anything in mind? Has he found out where the careers service is at uni? Does he know when the milk round is? (If you haven't been through this before, it's the name given to a set week during the university term when prospective employers visit the university and hold interviews.)

Use the holidays to help him find work experience. So he thinks he fancies law? A stint at a neighbour's office might confirm or dispel this idea. Either way, it's good experience (see section on holiday jobs).

YEAR OUT

If things aren't working out, a year out could be the answer. But make sure your student has discussed this fully with his tutor. A year might allow him to go back to a different course or just sort out any problems of his own before going back to the same.

The danger is, of course, that he might not go back. You can't ensure this doesn't happen, but you could steer him in the right direction. If he's having time off for emotional or medical problems, find expert help through your GP.

If he's taking time off because he wants to do a different course, try to help him spend that year wisely. Could he build up work experience? Is this a good time to go travelling? Don't let him waste it. He might not get this opportunity again.

GAP YEAR AFTER UNI

Gap years are coming full circle. In our day, we might – if we were lucky – have had a gap year after uni. Now, as we know, many students do it before. But that doesn't mean they can't do it afterwards too or instead of. Before you throw up your hands in horror at the prospect of having an unemployed student child for life, a gap year can give them the chance to think out their life. And isn't that better than going straight into a job that they might regret later on?

LANGUAGE YEAR OUT

Most language students have a year out abroad in their third year. But before you start panicking about the cost, there's a wonderful scheme called the Erasmus Exchange. Under this, students who go to continental Europe for their year get a grant of around 2,000 euros for the academic year. Even better, they don't have to pay any tuition fees.

If they want to go further afield, it could be costlier. For example, they usually have to pay 50 per cent of tuition fees in South America and there isn't a grant.

The good news is that they will have a fantastic time abroad. "We joke that it's four years for the price of three if they go to Europe," says a spokesperson for the International and Study Abroad Office at Sussex University. "Nearly all the students come back saying they've matured and really benefited."

It can also boost their love life. "Yes, we do get exchange couples when our students fall in love with someone abroad. Often this leads to a permanent relationship."

Well, so much for entering Europe...

CHAPTER TWENTY SIX

Exam stress

Try to find out from the bits of paper that might be lying round in your son's vacated bedroom when the exam period is. If you can't plough your way through the rubbish, it's time to do two things. Tidy up, and phone the uni for dates.

That way, you're prepared. So when you casually ask your daughter when her exams are, you can put her straight if she's not certain. Give her gentle reminders that build up to cattle prods during the lead up time. Is she revising? Does she know exactly when each exam is?

This might sound like spoon feeding but you'd be surprised how many students get this wrong. I know someone whose third year son thought his biology exam was on the following Friday. He was lying in bed, taking a well earned rest on the previous Thursday, when a friend knocked on the door and asked him how he'd answered the first question. Yes, he'd missed the exam. He was unable to graduate. And he had to go back the following autumn term to retake along with other students who'd missed it from being ill. It completely scuppered his career plans because he couldn't take up his new job. You have been warned.

On the other hand, if you have a panicker, you need to reassure them at the other end of the phone/computer. This might be the time for a comforting visit together with a parcel of goodies and a bottle of wine. Remind them that it's not the end of the world if it all goes wrong. Point out that, despite their fears, they're not going to sit in front of a blank piece of paper. There's bound to be *something* they can write about. Give them the kind of advice you gave them during A levels about pacing themselves/early nights/all that kind of boring stuff which is in fact essential.

PERSONAL STORY

"I rang my daughter just before her first year exams and I could tell from her voice that she was tearful," said Joanna from York. "I didn't want to probe too much because I thought she might burst into tears and I didn't think that would help. So I just told her that I know exams are horrible to go through but that once she found herself sitting in front of that paper, she would be fine. I also pointed out that if everything went wrong, the university had retakes in the summer. Showing her that there was a safety net, made it better."

TIP

Long before they take their finals – preferably in the first year – send them a brilliant book The Insider's Guide to Getting a First (or avoiding a Third) by Mark Black. It's packed with tips on how to get that ultimate grade, without being a geek. Published at £5.99 by White Ladder (yes, we think of everything) you can order it at **www.whiteladderpress.com**.

SURPRISE IN THE POST

When my son took his first year exams, I sent him a cake in the post to cheer him up. But when he was doing his second year exams, I forgot. He soon put me straight by casually mentioning in a phone call that it would be nice to get a parcel. The parents of all the other boys' in his house had apparently sent good luck cards and goodies in the post. I hadn't because I'd thought he didn't need it any more. Just goes to show how wrong you can get it. I promptly went down to the post office and sent, at great expense, two Jiffy bags of food essentials which would have been much cheaper for him to have bought at his local supermarket. But they tasted better when they arrived as a surprise parcel. All of which proves what we'd long suspected: kids are kids at heart even when they're grown up.

GIVE THEM A WAKE UP CALL

You could say the same about wake up calls. Yes, of course they're old enough to get themselves up for an exam. But what if they don't? Gillian from London has a (hopefully) failsafe system for her son who normally doesn't get up until at least midday. "I bought him four new alarm clocks which he sets at 10 minutes apart. I then ring him on his mobile and then again to make sure he's in the shower. Only then do I feel reasonably happy that he's going to make the exam."

Of course, there are diehards out there who would say that if a student can't get himself up for an exam, he's pretty hopeless and is unemployable. Absolutely right. But that doesn't stop us trying as parents, does it?

FIND OUT WHEN THE RETAKES ARE

Before the run up to the exams, gently find out what happens if they have to do retakes. Don't do this just before they're about to sit the paper, or it will deflate their confidence. Stuart from Bath didn't check his daughter's retake dates until he'd already booked the family holiday on which his daughter (astoundingly) had expressed interest in joining. "It was only after I paid the deposit that she told me it was during the retake period. She didn't know if she was going to have to do retakes at that time but it was an added worry when she took the exams because she knew she'd have to miss out on the holiday if she failed. We also felt lousy as parents because we would have had to have chosen between the holiday and being at home, checking she was OK about going back. In the end it was all right because she passed. But now we always check retake dates."

Also find out how they get their results. In our day, we had to queue up outside the faculty board. Now it's usually online and – during the first and second year – sometimes during the holidays. If they're going to be away, do they want you to log on and give them their grades? Do you really want to carry the can?

TWENTY SEVEN

Moving into a student house

It's the phone call we dread (well, one of them). "Mum, I don't want to stay in hall next year. I'm going into a house with friends."

When our son first said that, at the end of his first year, our immediate reaction was a) It will be too expensive b) How will he cook for himself? and c) They'll set the house on fire.

In fact, to our amazement, it has worked out well so far although we were right about a).

Some parents we know have actually forbidden their kids to move into a student house. This can be a big mistake. They're adults, after all, and they could lose friends – not to mention respect for you – if you stop them from entering an important rite of adult/student passage. If you're worried because you can't afford to fund them, make it clear that they're responsible for their own budget.

However, it's only sensible to get your student to consider the following points:

- How much is the rent? Get them to draw up a weekly budget, using figures from the previous occupants for gas/electricity bills and so on.

- Make an arrangement over phone bills with the others in the house. Ideally, have a ringing-in system only. They can use mobiles to call out so everyone is responsible for their own bill.

- How much is the deposit? What are the terms for it being refunded? Some crafty landlords try to claim damages and keep the deposit to pay for this. There are also apocryphal tales about landlord 'inspectors' creating holes in the wall and then charging for damage.

- What happens if something is broken? Do they have to replace it?

- Get someone (one parent is bound to be a lawyer) to check the tenancy agreement.

- Ideally, get an agreement which just covers the academic year. If you're still paying over the summer and your student is at home, it's a waste. It's also a good idea to pay for the rent by direct debit so you don't fall behind with rent and then have to pay a fine, depending on your agreement.

- Do they really like the friends they're moving in with? Unlike hall where they can shut themselves in their own room if they fall out with others, or just need some p and q, this is going to be more difficult in a student house.

- Do they realise they still need to work? Student houses can be noisy, often when some of the occupants need to get an essay finished even if the others have missed their deadlines.

- Where else can they work if the house is noisy? How far is the library and so on?

- How far is the house from lectures? Is it too far? What's the transport like?

At the end of term, make sure there's a cleaning rota so everyone does their bit in order to get back that elusive deposit. Consider paying a local cleaner to do a proper job. Some landlords make a video of the house before students move in so they know what it should look like. It's an idea for students also to take pictures with a camera to remind themselves.

Many landlords provide an inventory of how many chairs there are and pieces of cutlery and so on. This should also include any existing problems like a scratch on the kitchen table. Check this carefully with your student. Also look around and make sure there aren't any other defects which you haven't caused but which you might be charged for. A bit like checking a hired car before you go out in it.

Go over the fire regulations which should be provided by the agent. Legally, there should be smoke alarms and fire escapes. One student is normally nominated as fire officer. This basically means checking the alarms work.

Make sure your family insurance policy will cover your student's possessions. If not, sort this out.

TIPS

- Teach them how to put out a microwave fire: press the stop button. Don't open the door. Unplug it. Open the windows as smoke will come out of the vent at the back of the microwave. Close the door from the kitchen to the rest of the house. The fire should burn itself out within a few seconds but if not, call the fire brigade. (Advice taken from 'The Worst-Case Scenario Survival Handbook: University' £9.99. Chronicle Books. By Joshua Piven, David Borgenicht and Jennifer Worick)

- Teach them the meaning of sell-by dates and how to store food correctly in the fridge, eg raw food on different shelf from cooked.

FINDING A HOUSE

Most students start trying to do this in February or March. The trick, says my son and his mates, is to make friends with third or fourth years who've got enviable pads. Then see if you can move in when they go. Alternatively, sign up with an estate agent to find a house. Some estate agents may charge you for signing with them though; shop around and find one who won't charge.

Here are some more points to consider:

- Get your student to think twice about sharing a room. Very few people have the same work/sleep patterns.

- Are there locks on bedroom doors to protect your property even if one of your house mates leaves the front door open by mistake? If not, will the landlord let you put one on? Is the front door secure? Does everyone know how to work it? What are the rules if you lose the front door key? Most agents who handle leases charge for a spare.

- Are there enough computer points for internet access?

TIPS

- Draw up a list of chores so everyone does something. Point out that washing up is easier and less unpleasant if you do it on the same day instead of the next day or next week.

- Encourage them to take it in turns to cook. In our son's house, everyone cooked for the others one night a week, except at weekends when they did their own thing – in other words, fought over the tin opener/got a take away.

- Try to get them to avoid putting a deposit down on a house they think they like – and then losing it when they find one they prefer.

What every parent should know *before* their child goes to university

- Have fridge rules. Label food. Or have a rule where loo paper, milk and bread is communal.

- Check out communal facilities like food at the student union and visiting old halls as a guest for meals.

CHAPTER TWENTY EIGHT

Health – again

We've already brushed on this when your student first went to uni. But as the terms go by, it's still important to keep tabs on their well-being. Do they look pale? Are they constantly tired? Have they lost/gained weight dramatically? Are they thirstier than usual or do they go to the loo all the time? If you're concerned about these symptoms or anything else, encourage them to book an MoT with the GP.

TIP

Send them back with a good make of vitamin tablet.

WARNING: Students don't get free prescriptions automatically. They have to ask for a HCI form from the doctor's which entitles them to free prescriptions if they're on a low income. And most students are, aren't they?

MENTAL HEALTH

Joking apart, it can be a mental strain being a student. It's not all drink, drink, drink you know. Some students do work hard and they have too high expectations of themselves (which you might or might not be responsible for). Look out for danger signs like obsessive handwashing, bad temper (worse than usual), or talking in their sleep.

Contact the charity SANE for more advice on 0207 422 5556.

DENTIST

This is one thing you can keep an eye on. Book your student in to the family dentist during holidays. Hopefully this will instill a routine into him for later life. But be prepared for a shock – students aged 19 or over have to pay 80 per cent of NHS dental fees. Ask the dentist for an HCI form to fill in.

BODY CHECKS

Teach your student son to check his testicles regularly. Testicular cancer is more common than you might realise with teenagers and young men. Teach your daughter how to examine her breasts. If she needs guidance on this, encourage her to see the nurse at the medical centre or to book in at a Well Woman clinic. Also explain the importance of having regular smear tests.

CHAPTER TWENTY NINE

Term time jobs

TERM TIME JOBS

Here's a good one, with lots of potential for arguments. The plus of getting a job is that they'll have more money for drinking – sorry, hall fees. The downside is that it's bound to take up studying time and they'll be tired for exams/lectures, particularly if they're doing bar work.

So choose your side. Your student might want to work and you'll be worried about the effect on her work. Or you might say she should work and she'll say she can't find any.

A compromise is ideal but as any parent knows, compromises can only be reached through the equivalent of the United Nations. If possible, however, a small job which only takes up a couple of hours a week might teach some life skills to your student – and also provide a bit of extra beer money.

But be realistic. Some subjects really don't allow enough time for your student to get working. Medics, for example, are usually discouraged from getting jobs by their tutors because their timetable is already packed and it wouldn't be good for their health (or their patients if and when they eventually qualify) if they skimped on lectures for the sake of earning a few more quid.

HOLIDAY JOBS

Now this one is different. A holiday job is essential. It will give them something to put on their CV if they ever get as far as working in the real world. It will teach them that responsibility doesn't just mean offering to buy the next round in the pub. And it will help them to learn the value of money – in other words, that they can't just sponge off you in the holiday.

There's only one problem. Most holiday jobs are organised at least several weeks before the holidays start. And if your student isn't around to do this, he might well find they've all gone when he gets back. But don't panic. Here are the options:

- Investigate the job market on his behalf. Ring up local pubs/restaurants and explain your son is coming down in a few weeks. Enquire if there are any vacancies and see if they could interview him if he visited for the weekend before the end of term.

- Get him to enrol with a local recruitment consultant/agency. Contrary to popular student misconception, agencies often need students for short term temp work.

- Pick up a job form at your local supermarket some weeks before the end of term and send it to your student at uni. Make him fill it in by threatening to withdraw his grant.

- Get him to advertise his services locally. Not *those* kind of services. Babysitting, gardening, house sitting etc. Anything that fits in with his own social commitments such as holidays.

- Encourage him to find a more interesting job. Au pair agencies are now taking more short term au pairs, just for the holidays. Bunac runs Camp America and needs students to help on American camps. They pay for the flight and accommodation and the student gets pocket money in return – and the chance to see another continent.

Get him to use holiday time to find out what he might like to do when he finally leaves uni. Ring your contacts to arrange a spell in a legal department/fashion store/school etc.

IMPORTANT FACT

Tell your son what the minimum wage is so he's not fobbed off with peanuts by unscrupulous employers. For 18 – 21 year olds (and over 22 year olds if they receive accredited training for six months after they start work) it's known as the Minimum Wage Development Rate and it's currently £4.10 an hour. For more details, contact the National Minimum Wage helpline on 0845 600 0678.

TIPS

- Check the employer's stance on tax. Some bosses will charge students tax and then your offspring will have to go through the rigmarole of getting forms from the tax office to reclaim it as students don't have to pay tax. Mind you, that's probably the next thing to go....

- Also get your student to agree basics in writing with their employer such as working hours and holidays. If the employer doesn't stick to the agreement, talk to the local citizens Advice Bureau or the firm's union rep.

MUM! DAD! I'M BROKE!

A friend of mine always knows roughly how much her daughter

has in her account because the bank statements are still sent to the home address and the daughter hasn't yet had them changed to the uni address. Yes, the friend does know she shouldn't open the statements but she argues that as it's *her* money that her daughter is spending, she's entitled to know if she's overdrawn.

Not all of us would go that far but, just as it's important to work out a budgeting strategy with your student, so it's important to work out what she should do if she exceeds her limit. And what better time to have this heart to heart than in the holidays when she could get a holiday job to make up for the money she's squandered.

Ideally, get her to come clean with you. Better that than build up debts which come as a shock to you when you eventually find out about them and which worry her to the extent that it affects her work.

PERSONAL STORIES

"When our son admitted he was overdrawn by £800 three weeks before the end of term, we said we'd cover him if he worked during the holiday and paid us back," said one father who didn't want to be identified. "It worked and because he had very little money left for himself, he didn't get overdrawn again."

But not every parent can afford to top up their child. "We went to see the bank manager together," said another mother who was in this situation. "He was quite tough and said my son needed to be more careful. But he did extend his overdraft on condition that he worked during the holidays and paid it off. Later, we sat down and went through his weekly expenses and worked out how to cut corners.

He reduced the number of times he went out during the week and started cooking more for himself instead of getting take aways. He also used the second hand book shop on the campus instead of buying books new online. Or else he bought second hand online. He hadn't realised you could do that."

TIP

Get them to stop using their credit card. Use cheques instead or, even better, cash. It hurts more when you're buying something to hand over notes – and it makes you think about whether you really need it.

CHAPTER THIRTY

How to deal with broken hearts

They might not tell you but the signs are there. Depressed sounding voice, filthy mood, not wanting to eat – all the things you've been coping with since they were 13. Seriously, a broken heart at uni is hard for a parent to deal with if they're a long way off. And even if they're not, your student will probably think you wouldn't understand anyway.

The only way to deal with this is to make it clear that you're there if they need you. Try not to be too judgmental. If you tell your daughter you've always loathed her ex, it's tricky when she gets back together with him.

"It's tempting to jump in the car and go and see her immediately,'" says Denise Knowles, counsellor for Relate. "But if you can't, a listening ear and a cuddle down the phone is vital. Let them cry and then ask what she would like you to do now. Does she want to come home or does she want you to come up next weekend? Give her options. It will make her feel as though there is hope – which, of course, there is."

If your child doesn't want to open up to you, perhaps it's time to respect her need for privacy. Or you could carry on being interfering and visit with tempting goodies and talk about normal things on the phone. That way, you might coax or tempt her into confiding. Remind her of friends who have gone through the same thing or of previous relationships that went wrong before she found happiness again. If she can't talk to you, maybe she could talk to a brother or sister or friend at home.

Similarly, try to point out – without preaching – the moral protocol of life. It's not kind to drop someone without explanation. It usually doesn't bring happiness if you sleep with a different person every week. Hopefully, these are principles that they will have already absorbed during teenage life. But university life can change people when they realise the vast possibilities of a social life that they didn't have at home.

This is a short chapter because, sometimes, there is nothing you can do when their heart is broken. It's part of life and you went through it yourself. Second thoughts, you could tell them about that. It might make them smile through the tears.

CHAPTER THIRTY ONE

Breaking the law

A new environment with new friends can change people – and not always for the better. Mike, the father of a 20 year old second year student, was horrified when his son rang from a police station to say he'd been charged with shoplifting at a local supermarket. "He said he'd done it because he'd run out of food and needed to eat. I felt terrible – firstly because I hadn't realised he was so short of money, and secondly because he had broken the law."

The case went to court and the student was fined. He now has a record and – just as bad – very low self-esteem which is affecting his work.

"We've never been the kind of family to get into trouble with the law," said Mike. "And I didn't expect my son to do anything wrong. The awful thing is that I don't know how I could have stopped it. We spoke every fortnight or so on the phone and he didn't give me any indication that anything was wrong."

Sometimes you have to accept that your student is an adult. He has his own life to lead, and you can't always make sure he's on the straight and narrow. You can, however, give him basic principles and reinforce these when you see him.

Also try to meet his friends. You can't get him to change them if you disapprove but you can give him gentle pointers. Friends are extremely influential in a limited world like university and can be responsible for people behaving well or badly.

Talk through legal issues before your child goes to university. Point out that cannabis is still illegal and that they can go to jail for taking it. Encourage them to confide in you if they run short of money before they do anything illegal to bump up their bank account.

Also talk rape. This isn't easy – but it's something that male students need to be aware of. He has to be certain that a girl wants sex too or he could be accused of rape. Similarly, talk to your daughter. Point out the dangers of crying wolf. It's not pleasant but it has to be done.

WHERE TO FIND HELP

If your child has been accused of breaking the law, find a good solicitor and also contact his personal tutor. The university needs to be aware of the situation and might be more sympathetic than you think. Also talk to the counselling services at uni.

AGAINST THE RULES

You might not have a jailbird student. But most students break the rules at some point in their university life. One friend was appalled at finding a letter from the hall warden – which her son had proudly displayed on his bedroom wall. It informed him that he and some friends had been cautioned by the warden because they had 'borrowed' a series of road signs which they had then taken back to their rooms. Unfortunately for them, the cleaning lady – who did her bit every fortnight in their rooms – spilt the beans. The signs were duly returned and a comment was no doubt made in the hall record book. My friend duly gave her son a pep talk (during which my her husband confessed to doing the same thing some 25 odd years ago at uni) and, to their knowledge, this hasn't happened again. It might not seem that serious but it could have been the start of something bigger. Maybe all students need to go through this in order for it to be pointed out that enough is enough.

CHAPTER THIRTY TWO

Graduation

It hardly seems any time at all since you took your student up to uni for fresher week. And now it's graduation. In fact, three years isn't that long – something perhaps that we should all have pointed out when they started.

WHAT KIND OF A DEGREE?

Of course it sounds great to tell everyone that your son or daughter got a First or 2:1. But that's not what university is all about. Good grades are a help when it comes to some jobs and a First or good 2:1 is usually essential for a PHd. But you'd be surprised at how many employers even bother with the final grade or ask what employees got. They're far more concerned with the whole picture and what your offspring are like as people.

So don't impose your own expectations on your student. They didn't go to university to make up for what you didn't do – or to do as well as you did. The vital point is that university has been a fantastic stepping stone between school and real life.

"I have made an effort. I'm wearing a tie aren't I?"

THE CEREMONY

This can be fun – providing you know what's going on. Remember the days when you missed speech day or sports day because your primary school child didn't give you the note at the bottom of his bag? Well, graduation can be a bit like that. Drum out of her what time you're meant to be where, and how many guests you can bring.

Check what he's meant to be wearing. Has he hired his gown in time? Does he need a mortar board? He might have a degree but that doesn't mean he has learned to dress himself. (It should be said here that my husband who graduated from Cardiff in the seventies, had to borrow a friend's gown because he forgot to get his own. This required a complicated pantomime of antics in which his friend crossed the stage to receive his degree certificate and then had to dash backstage to hand his gown to my husband.)

Try, also, to be reasonably polite to your ex if you are both going to be at the graduation. Anna, now 25, says her graduation was ruined by her mother spitting at her father's new wife during most of the ceremony. This is their day – not yours. Save the rancour for phone calls and solicitors' letters.

CHAPTER THIRTY THREE

Hi! I'm back!

This is the ultimate irony. You wept when they left for uni. You've spent three years making sure they didn't run up a huge overdraft or break the law. You've tried to make sure they've worked hard enough for a decent degree and you've tried not to be hurt when they didn't ring when they said they would.

And now they're coming home to live with you again – just as you've worked out a life of your own. More 20 and 30 somethings now live with their parents than ever before. This isn't just a tribute to your cooking; it's also because they're too broke to have a home of their own.

Think carefully before you say yes. You and your graduate have both done a lot of growing up over the years. You're not the same people. Are you both ready to make the compromises that being back together under one roof is going to demand?

How about starting with a trial period? (A bit like living together before you get married or, in this case, before you throw them out.) Suggest a reasonable period like three months and see how it works out. Draw up a budget and make it clear that your graduate has to contribute to living expenses. At least this will be an incentive to getting a job. Talking of which…

HELPING THEM FIND A JOB

Does this parenting stuff ever end? You've got them through school, you've mortgaged them through university and now they need pushing to get a job.

Encourage them with relevant newspaper vacancies. Suggest local employment agencies and ring up friends who might be able to help. Point out that they might not get what they want immediately but that experience goes a long way. Help them draw up a CV.

PERSONAL STORY

Don't panic if they come home without having secured a job on the milkround. This doesn't mean they're never going to work. "Neither of our two children got a job immediately after graduating," says Kim, a mother from Lancaster. "We told them not to panic but at the same time, we went down to the library and the careers office and trawled the net with them. Now our daughter is in advertising and our son is a teacher. They both love their jobs – even though my son didn't think of teaching until he'd been in a boring job for a year and did a rethink. My advice is not to panic but, at the same time, to be there when they do."

CHAPTER THIRTY FOUR

Foreign and mature students

If you're based abroad and your son or daughter wants to come to a British university, log on to **www.ucas.com/studyuk/ what.html**. This will give you a basic run down on how long degree courses last, how much they will cost, and what qualifications your child needs.

If English isn't your child's first language, most unis and colleges will require a qualification in English or ask your child to take a specified test in English to show they can cope with their studies. It goes without saying that your child also needs a valid passport to come to the UK.

MATURE STUDENTS

It might well be that you feel so envious of your student offspring that you're tempted to do a degree yourself. In fact, why not go the whole hog and go to the same uni so you can *really* embarrass them?

UCAS publishes a helpful leaflet on how to go about this (doing a mature degree, that is – not going to the same uni, necessarily). It's called *The Mature Students' Guide to Higher Education*. It includes sections on choosing what to study, qualifications (which are often lower for mature students than you might think), childcare and finance. For example, if you are aged under 50, you can still apply for a student loan. So get in there fast. (Details are on our website at **www.whiteladderpress.com**.)

This could be your chance to go to Oxford or Cambridge. The Kellogs College at Oxford, for example, specialises in mature students.

CONTACTS

You'll find a listing of other helpful contacts at **www.whiteladderpress.com** alongside the information about this book.

CHAPTER THIRTY FIVE

Learn from our mistakes – and the things we got right

TALES FROM PARENTS WHO'VE BEEN THROUGH IT – AND SOME WHO ARE STILL GOING THROUGH IT

Patrick and Jill, from Amersham, have one third-year son at Bristol and one first year at Warwick.

- We keep in touch through the web. Nick has set up a weblog which is a diary on the internet. He tells us what he's been doing and we add our comments to it. For us, it works better than a phone call because it's more spontaneous. The trick is to communicate with young people in the way they like best. We also have webcams so we can have video conferences through the computer. It makes them feel less isolated. Even though they've got lots of friends, they still like talking to us – which is nice.

- We also have a roof box to put on top of the roof rack when we take them to uni. It gives you that extra room.

- When our second son left for university, we thought we'd feel really strange without children in the house any more. In fact, it was easier than we'd thought. I think this was because we found it harder when the first one went (Jill cried). But we knew that after a week or so you began to get used to it.

It helped that by the time the second went, we were working in the family business together. My advice to other couples? Do things together and be patient with each other. Look at the advantages. You're not going to be woken up in the middle of the night by the sound of the car or the front door opening. You don't have to cook dinner at odd times. Food lasts longer in the fridge. You haven't got to live with mood swings (unless you have them). It's easy to communicate with them.

- When it comes to budgeting, we pay hall fees and tuition. Then we work out what we consider to be a reasonable amount, depending on their accommodation (one is in self-catering and the other is catered for) and books etc. We give each of them £50 a week. We haven't had to top up until this term but now we've got to because one of our sons went on a field trip and linked his mobile phone into the net. Vodaphone contacted us to see if we realised he'd run up a £200 bill in one month.

- We do get our boys to work in the holidays and save the money towards pocket money for term time.

- When they've been ill, we haven't gone racing up in the first week but given them advice about drinking (not alcohol) and paracetamol. But we did go up after 10 days when one of our sons was still ill with tonsillitis. Our advice is not to fuss but be aware.

- Keep talking to your children even if you fall out. They need you as a sounding board, however old they are.

Sally and John from Colchester have three daughters at uni.

- If they get ill, suggest they buddy up with a friend who can make sure they're alright the next day and can check them in the morning. Try to get them to do this after a night of partying, too.

- Make sure they've had a meningitis jab before starting uni.

- Teach them to use a reputable local taxi service that's registered. People assume taxis are safe but that's not always true.

- Bikes can be really useful if your student has a long way to walk to lectures. Try to get them to wear a helmet and try out the route first.

- Before trying to cram a bike in the car, see if there's a local bike company that hires out bikes at an affordable termly rate. There usually is. Make sure it's checked for safety. Don't suggest they get a moped unless they're used to one.

- If they're taking the car, teach them to park under a street light. Don't take a smart car or it might get vandalised – and they're bound to have a knock. Buy them a crook lock.

- Pay a set amount of money into their account once a month instead of giving it to them in one go.

- Don't assume your son has to have a credit card. He can validate cheques with another kind of card. A credit card might encourage him to spend more.

- Talk about the importance of not running up an overdraft. It doesn't matter if everyone else does it.

- If it's not too late, think about how far the uni is – and how you'd get there. Some children think they'll be fine to be a long way from home and then find it difficult when they get there. On the other hand, a uni that seems a long way off might have good transport connections. For example, you can fly cheaply to certain Scottish universities.

- If they're homesick in the first few weeks, reassure them that they'll feel better soon and that it *will* pass.

- Teach them to lock the room even if they're in the kitchen or bathroom at the end of the corridor. One of our daughter's friends had her laptop stolen when she went to make a cup of coffee.

- Send them off with a batch of discs so they can back up their computer work. Teach them to do it at the end of every day.

- If they're on the ground floor and you're concerned about safety, talk to the warden.

Dr Pat Spungin, mother of two graduates and one undergrad. Founder of www.raisingkids.co.uk *which gives advice to parents.*

- Sometimes take family friends to visit your student children. It can make a visit less intense. Children can find it hard to entertain parents on their home ground and a visitor gives everyone a distraction.

- Feed them up during these visits – and when they come home. If there's one thing that students look forward to when they see parents, it's a good meal. Stock up the fridge before they get back and don't complain when they help themselves. They're used to freedom now. At the same time, they need to understand that you might have put that ham aside for a particular meal...

- Take lots of bin liners when you pick them up at the end of term. They're bound not to have packed everything and they can fit in small spaces in the car where suitcases can't.

- Teach your student basic cookery before they go. Home made soups are very easy. Buy them a small electric blending/chopping appliance for puréeing vegetables for soup.

What every parent should know *before* their child goes to university

- Encourage them to make meals at home when they're back, to show you what they've learned. It's good for their confidence and it gives you a break.

Karen and Matt from London have a son who's in his second year at Sheffield

- He spent his first year in hall and the advice the uni sent out before he started suggested taking a drying rack. It's been a brilliant idea and he still uses it now he's in a house. You just put it up near the radiator and it makes sure they don't wear damp clothes. You don't need to iron either – at least that's what he says.

- We also send him up with a couple of extension leads. There are never enough points in a room for all their electric kit.

Michele Eliott, director of the charity Kidscape, has two graduate sons

- Tell them they don't have to stay at uni if they hate it. This gives them the freedom to talk to you and say if something is wrong. There are too many suicide attempts and suicides by bright kids at uni who have felt pressure from family to make a success of it.

- When packing, only take the bare minimum until you see what they need. Both my boys took way too much stuff and could hardly move in their dorm rooms. We ended up by bringing lots back.

- Teach them how to bake a potato, fry eggs and how to get by without eating out every day. Show them a budget which involves a meal or two out (say £10-£15) and multiply it by a week or month so they can get the whole picture. Eating in and getting coffee (beer) out with friends, means more money to spend on fun things.

• Encourage them to join lots of clubs and societies and try them out – but not to commit themselves until they've seen their work schedule.

• Get them to ask for help the first time they fall behind with work. Explain they shouldn't kid themselves that they'll catch this up. The further behind they get, the less likely they are to ask for help and then it is often too late. Professors are usually understanding if you don't leave it too long.

Katrina has two daughters, one who is in her third year at London and another who graduated from London two years ago.

• As well as emailing, I regularly send funny postcards and cards. They love getting things in the post and it's more personal than email. Before they go off at the beginning of term, we go shopping and get a great hamper of food. It's comforting for them to have things they like to eat, even if they're catered for at hall.

• We took out the loan but banked it and the girls used the interest as pocket money. I appreciate not many can do this but it's nice if you can.

• Take storage boxes – like the ones on wheels from John Lewis – to go under the bed to store extra clothes. But check the bed before you buy them as some beds don't have the space underneath.

• Encourage them to eat pasta, fruit and jacket potatoes.

• Buy a window alarm for their window if they're on the ground floor.

- If they're in a rented house, supply them with carbon monoxide detectors and spare smoke alarms. Make sure the house conforms to safety standards. You can get a list of requisites from the local authority. If something is missing like a smoke alarm, contact the landlord.

- Pack a torch and spare batteries even if they're in hall.

- If they're not working hard enough, try to motivate them by pointing out what they could achieve if they do work. Sometimes you have to wait until they realise this themselves. If they moan about not enjoying part of their courses, point out that this is life.There will always be bits they don't like but then they'll find work they do enjoy.

- Stop worrying. You can't do anything about how late they're going to stay up or what they're going to do. You have to let go at 18.

Gael Lindenfield, psychotherapist and author including Confident Teens, Thorsons £9.99. Gael had two daughters who went to university, both of whom changed courses. Tragically one of them died. **www.gaellindenfield.com**.

- Both my daughters changed courses after finding they didn't like them. We didn't insist they carried on but supported them in trying to find courses that suited them better. Sadly, Laura died before she could start her second course. Our other daughter approached universities directly instead of going through UCAS and was accepted for a course that she really enjoyed. But they did have friends whose parents insisted they continued even though they hated it. I think that's a shame. Once they've learned from one mistake, they're more likely to choose carefully next time.

- Even though my daughter was five hours away from home, I

would meet her just for coffee or lunch instead of the whole day. That could be too intense for some students – they have busy lives. A coffee or light lunch is more casual and can lead to more communication than if they think 'I've got mum for the whole day. What am I going to do with her?'

Jackie from Suffolk has two children at university

- Teach them to budget at home so they're prepared when they go to uni. Be strong if they run out. We've just refused to top up one of our children and said she'll have to work to pay off her overdraft. It's not easy but if you don't, they don't learn. One of our friends pays a monthly sum to her son's account instead of giving him the loan all at once.

- Ring up at odd times to find out if they're working or partying.

- Check their bank balances if they come to the house. I don't think it's invading their privacy. You could then say to them 'Did you realise you've got such and such a sum left in your account?' They might be pleased because it could help them confide in you about money worries, and you can see if they've run up a big sum in a bar because they usually pay by card.

- Don't nag them about exams but ring them up quite a bit beforehand and casually ask how many more days they've got until exams start.

- Communicate, communicate, communicate! There's no excuse not to nowadays, with email and phone and texting. Also send parcels and letters.

- Give them a wok for cooking. They can do almost anything in it.

- Send them up with a spare supply of ink for the printer.

What every parent should know *before* their child goes to university

- If moving to a house, get the landlord's email address in case there are problems and you can't get hold of the agency.

CHAPTER THIRTY SIX

Fascinating facts you might not know about uni to impress your kids

- Graduates earn around £400,000 more than non-graduates during their working life. Pity you might not be around for them to share that with you.

- Once your child graduates, they could expect to earn around £18,000 in their first job. They're also half as likely to be unemployed as the rest of the nation. In other words, they should stop ringing you up and asking for handouts.

- Melinda Messenger apparently plans to enrol on a part time degree course at Reading University while continuing with her career. "A good education improves our chances of achieving the exciting joy you aspire to, let alone a better salary." Let's just hope that Reading Uni is ready for a rush of applications from male students.

- A graduate should never be lonely (apart from the first few scary weeks). "Think about the number of people you know at work, then multiply that by 2,000," says Aimhigher. "That's how many people most students can hope to meet on their course, at societies and clubs, in their halls of residence and at the student coffee bar."

- 300,000 young people go into higher education every year.

What every parent should know *before* their child goes to university

- Seventy-seven per cent of ex-students say it kick-started their ambition and determination. The rest are still at the bar. (Sadly, not the legal variety.)

- There are 50,000 different courses on offer at uni and college. Many are vocational and include Sports Coaching, Photography and Hotel Management. So they don't need to be a whizz at maths or more traditional subjects.

- Ninety-seven per cent of ex-students never regret their college experience. Would the remaining three per cent write to us, please? It might make another book.

Conclusion

Exhausted? We know how you feel. By the time you've finally got them off to uni, you'll feel as though you've completed a degree yourself. The bad news is that you still feel pretty shattered every time you pack them up and send them back for a new term. The good news is that it gets easier because you've learned so much (rather like giving birth again and again and again). And there's also the added bonus that by the time they finally graduate they will, hopefully, have become more rounded, capable citizens who can grill a rasher of bacon as well as writing a thesis on 17th century French politics. After that, all they need to do is find a job…

Useful contacts

You'll find an extensive list of websites, books and contact addresses for students and their families on our website. Go to **www.whiteladderpress.com** and you'll find it alongside the information about this book. Posting the information on the website allows us to keep it updated. Please let us know of any other contact details which should be added to the list. Thanks.

Contact us

You're welcome to contact White Ladder Press if you have any questions or comments for either us or the author. Please use whichever of the following routes suits you.

Phone: **01803 813343**

Email: **enquiries@whiteladderpress.com**

Fax: **01803 813928**

Address: **White Ladder Press, Great Ambrook, Near Ipplepen, Devon TQ12 5UL**

Website: **www.whiteladderpress.com**

What can our website do for you?

If you want more information about any of our books, you'll find it at **www.whiteladderpress.com**. In particular you'll find extracts from each of our books, and reviews of those that are already published. We also run special offers on future titles if you order online before publication. And you can request a copy of our free catalogue.

Many of our books also have links pages, useful addresses and so on relevant to the subject of the book. You'll also find out a bit more about us and, if you're a writer yourself, you'll find our submission guidelines for authors. So please check us out and let us know if you have any comments, questions or suggestions.

Would you like your child to get a top degree?

If so, you could do worse than give them a copy of *The Insider's Guide to Getting a First (or avoiding a Third)*...

Only a fraction over 10 per cent of students get a First class degree. Hard work helps but it's no guarantee and it's, well... hard work. So what's the alternative?

The answer is strategy. The kind of strategy that saves you a lot of the hard slog, gives you time to go out with your mates in the evenings, and still gets you a top degree at the end of the course. And just such a strategy has now been devised.

Mark Black was an average student getting average grades. He took a law degree and earned a 2:2. Perfectly respectable but nothing special. Then, at the age of 22, he decided to take an MBA. When he realised he was 10 years younger than almost everyone on the course (apart from his twin brother Stephen) he could see he was headed for humiliation. In order to avoid this he developed a strategy to keep him in the running. To his surprise, his strategy did better than that: it put him top of his course at the end of the first term. He honed his approach and, by the end of the next term, he had extended his lead. After his final term and his dissertation, he finished top of his course with a Distinction (equivalent to a First).

Rather than keep the secret to himself, Mark reveals his successful strategy in *The Insider's Guide to* **Getting A First** *(or avoiding a Third)* available from us at £5.99 (p&p free). To give you a taster, here's an extract from the book.

STRATAGEM 8: TEAMWORK

Teamwork helped both me and my brother get Distinctions. It's that simple. To do it alone is a very difficult task and you need to have a lot of talent and commitment. Why not make it easier? If you split the workload and help each other out then you can free up time to enjoy yourself and relax.

We used the fact that we were twins to our advantage. As a first example, we split the reading list. Each week we'd read half of what we'd been told to read in full. As we had six modules per semester, this usually entailed me doing the reading for three of the modules in full while Stephen did the reading for the other three, and then we'd alternate modules every week.

But surely you're missing half the reading each week? Not so. Because we owned the books, we read each book armed with a highlighter and pen and we would highlight the important points while at the same time making little comments where a good thought had popped up. Then we could speed read the highlighted books from the other three modules each week and get the gist of what was being said.

This saved an enormous amount of time and was one of the ways in which we fully justified investing the money in our own copies of the books. We got all the understanding with about 60% of the effort compared with other students who were spending relentless hours trying to keep up. Frankly, to do our reading list alone would be impossible in my opinion. It was massive. I fully recommend that you get a partner on your course for this specific reason. Sharing the workload makes sense.

Share the research

We also split the research tasks. There was no point in us both going out and spending time trying to find the same articles. We alternated that as well. Each week I'd do the research for three modules while Stephen did the other three. This again had the effect that we were actually doing less work than the others and looking far better prepared than anybody else.

Add to this the fact that we'd bought broadband and our research was more productive in any case, and you start to see how the benefits snowball. Also consider that because we had strong relationships with the other students we were getting their research as well, and you start to see how the plan fits together to put us in a much better position than trying to do it as a one man mission, John Rambo style.

One of the key ways we split the research was on the actual assignments themselves. As well as knowing intricately what topic the other was doing, and so being able to look out for articles that would be useful, we gave each other the reference lists on assignments where we'd both been given the same task. This made our preparation for writing the essays much more effective.

Read each other's work

And once we'd written the assignments, we read each other's work and were able to give an informed but independent opinion about how to improve each other's essay. Several times we would catch gaps in essays; things that were missing which needed to be in but had been overlooked.

On one occasion we'd been given a task that was open to interpretation, but we needed to address three key models. For whatever reason, the third model had been overlooked on one of Stephen's essays. Everyone makes mistakes so you need to have procedures in place to catch them. Quality assurance, really.

In this particular case I only spotted it while we were printing out my essay to hand it in. Stephen quickly made the changes to include the comment needed on the third model and ended up receiving 81% for that particular essay. Without having caught the oversight, he wouldn't have been able to get a First because he'd have missed out a crucial part. Teamwork makes a difference.

The more people you can get involved in this process the better. For our dissertations there were three of us reading each other's essays. Two independent brains are better than one. In the preparation for our first exam there were six of us sitting round a table going through everyone's preparation to be sure that no one had overlooked the obvious. This was a great situation.

Getting a good mark has a lot to do with making sure that you haven't missed the obvious in any aspect. Don't make fundamental errors and you can't go far wrong. These meetings helped us eliminate those fundamental errors so that at least we all had a chance. It doesn't standardise everyone, it just ensures that everyone's still in the game. That included me so I ran with it.

To state the point again: teamwork helped us both get Distinctions. Too often the students who are trying to get Firsts are very secretive people. They play the game close to their chests and don't give much away. That's one way to do it but it wasn't our way. Our way is *much much* easier. It really is a situation where the end result will be more than the sum of the parts. I haven't made many express recommendations to you but I strongly suggest that you take this point on board. John Rambos don't come along very often. The rest of us do it together.

Index